ROSE

OF KINGSTON

the making of a theatre

'Who would have thought that a copy of Shakespeare's Rose in modern guise would be built at Kingston, just because a group of Kingstonians wanted it? It's absolutely crazy. If someone had told you that, you'd say – don't be silly; that'll never happen'.

Peter Hall

'There's a divinity that shapes our ends, Rough-hew them how we will'.

Shakespeare: *Hamlet*

Cover design courtesy of Martin Alton

The author acknowledges the invaluable assistance of Geoff Howard and Roger Chown in preparing this book for publication.

ISBN 978-1-916838-25-3

Printed in Great Britain by
Biddle Books Limited, King's Lynn, Norfolk

Dedication

This book is dedicated to all the people and organisations whose support and commitment over many decades turned the vision of a theatre in Kingston to the reality of The Rose, a theatre of national standing. It is also dedicated to all the volunteers and committed staff in a huge range of roles without whom The Rose would not be able to open its doors.

With best wishes,

Frank Whately

February 2024

Contents

1
A Trace of History

On the 16th January 2008 there was a sense of barely restrained elation in the auditorium of the Rose Theatre as the inaugural production opened. It was a preview of Chekhov's *Uncle Vanya*, directed by Peter Hall. There was also a sense of expectation which gave way to a spontaneous outburst of applause as the lights dimmed. Kingston finally had its theatre.

A week later the theatre.establishment flocked to Kingston for the official opening and press night. As Paul Taylor said in *The Independent*, 'If a bomb had dropped on the opening night, it would have wiped out a high percentage of Britain's theatrical bigwigs'. The Rose – and its first production – garnered reviews of unrestrained approval. Michael Billington, in *The Guardian*, wrote of the 'seductively handsome space'. Charles Spencer in *The Daily Telegraph* called the Rose 'a palpable hit' and an 'outstanding project'.

But this playhouse, before its fit-out, whilst still mere bricks and mortar, had already seen the sweep of action. Five years earlier in the spring of 2003, in a bare theatre 'shell', Barrie Rutter was the first professional actor to enter, from upstage, as the Chorus in his own Northern Broadsides production of *Henry V*. In the week before that the community play *Don Juan In Kingston* and a new Kingston audience had come together in some sort of consummation of the town's flirtation with plays and playing. This 2003 season in the shell was so important in a variety of ways. First and foremost it brought the reality of the theatre – much talked about for decades past – to Kingston. There was the sight of large theatre audiences leaving Kingston late at night, chilled to the marrow after three hours in an unheated amphitheatre, but smiling and talking, programmes tucked under arms: this was not only a social detail, but a fulfillment of a political aspiration to change Kingston at night.

A year later, still without the means to fund the final fit-out, the building was again filled by audiences hungry for Shakespeare. This time it was a revival of Peter Hall's *As You Like It*. Hall was, by then, Artistic Director of the Rose Theatre, Kingston. Surely the opening of the finished theatre could not be far away. Kingston audiences, and many from further afield, were delighted: Kingston felt like a changed place. However, four years – four rather long and taxing, sometimes static or certainly stop-start years – were to pass before that January opening night and Chekhov's masterpiece about hope and frustration.

But to put things in perspective, if one could cut back to Kingston in the early nineteen seventies a not-altogether different impression might have been given as a much smaller audience spilled out of the tiny Overground theatre onto Ashcroft Road near the Fairfield. Or just over one hundred years ago, an earlier generation of Kingstonians might have been seen leaving the newly opened Kingston Empire Theatre, in Clarence Street. Or a decade before that, in the year of Victoria's Jubilee, others still left the Royal County Theatre in Fife Road for the first time one October evening. Kingston has had an enduring relationship with theatre, both real and desired. And what does that go to show? That communities wait and wait and when they get it they take it for a while then pass on? That theatres don't last? That we outgrow our toys? That theatres are expensive baubles? As for the Rose, not everyone wanted it, nor did it elicit approval from everyone: a cursory glance through the letters column of the local newspaper, *The Surrey Comet*, in the critical years immediately before and after the Rose opening, reveals that while there was a great enthusiasm from many quarters, there was also some dissent, along with the inevitable vitriol from Brassed-off of Berrylands engaging the full repertoire of anti-arts dogma.

The names Kingston has given its playhouses at different times – the Royal County, the Empire, the Overground – are reflective of attitudes and aspirations, national preoccupations and deference. Whilst the Rose by any other name would smell as sweet, would it not still have what in its youthful state it was associated with? It is a place of beauty, if not complete perfection – an aspiration always associated with theatres and theatre productions, but rarely achieved; a place where good things can flourish and procreate; a place which attracts a wide diversity of people from all ages and walks of life. It has already brought pleasure and no small amount of pride, as well as plenty of panning and disparagement. For this particular building, though, it is with its historical antecedent that comparison should be made: a little amphitheatre erected on the south side of the Thames, across the water from, and so outside, the medieval city walls of London in 1587. It is here that the special qualities of Kingston's Rose can be seen in relief.

The decision in late twentieth century Kingston to squeeze a polygonal auditorium, measuring seventy three feet and seven inches in diameter onto a footprint – almost literally a boot shape – of land was decried by some as foolish. When that decision was made in 1998 even a few closely involved with the campaign to build a theatre questioned the idea. Indeed, one or two members of the Kingston Theatre Trust fell away: a space with the dimensions and characteristics of a long-lost antecedent was not their idea of a theatre. They had a clear notion of proscenium arches, rich red curtains and plush seats in the stalls or dress circle. After all, what Frank Matcham had given so many London Theatres a hundred years before – as well as to Richmond just up the road – had served their communities of theatre-goers perfectly well, so why should a modern equivalent not serve ours? Why decide to try and ape the design – in stage shape and relationship with the auditorium – of a playhouse knocked together somewhat haphazardly over four hundred years ago amongst the bawdy houses and gambling dens of a London suburb? Was this an attempt by Kingston to assert relationship with the greatest of the great theatre practitioners, Shakespeare? Just as Kingston's Victorian forebears had claimed association with the seven Saxon kings, so we were re-creating 'Shakespeare's theatre', the theatre where 'many of Shakespeare's plays were performed', the stage on which Shakespeare 'very probably' performed. As with the Saxon kings, the unaccredited claims were tenuous anyway: only one of Shakespeare's plays, *Titus Andronicus*, was certainly performed at the original Rose, and possibly a second in one part of *Henry V1* – but which part or all we know not. But it makes for a national narrative to talk of 'Shakespeare's Rose', and publicity merchants can happily be loose with the truth.

None of us who began to campaign for a theatre in Kingston can pretend that we had a clear vision which we followed through to the opening. The distinctive quality of what emerged is still being realised: directors and their productions are building on a body of performance work, responding to the special nature of the space; actors are adapting, with varying degrees of proficiency, to the opportunities which such a stage offers. Trevor Nunn, for instance, had often come to the Rose as it was developing and had for long harboured the desire to direct a production on the stage. When the opportunity arose, he chose with a nice sense of what might be appropriate: in the Autumn of 2015, he took on three plays, a reworking of the Royal Shakespeare Company's *Wars of the Roses*, which did so much to establish that company in the nineteen sixties. The resulting performances of *Henry V1*, *Edward 1V* and *Richard 111* were a triumph in the Rose space.

The discovery of the archaeology of the original Elizabethan Rose, built on the Southbank of the Thames in the year before the Spanish Armada came to be, in the end, our inspiration: the archaeological find, in 1989, excited imaginations all over the world, caused controversy and debate in Parliament and rallied members of the theatre establishment to protect the site. In Kingston, it did not go unnoticed and certainly, I was one of those who was stirred by the possibilities. But we were already pursuing our own campaign several years before that wonderful discovery close to Southwark Bridge.

Elizabethan and Jacobean theatre, both plays and history, had long fed much of my work as a teacher of English and Drama at Tiffin School in Kingston. My students were enthusiastic companions at the RSC's uncomfortable Aldwych theatre in London and miserable Memorial Theatre in Stratford. There were other personal promptings and provocations: the success of the recently opened Swan Theatre at Stratford upon Avon, in 1985, was evident. The Swan was designed by Michael Reardon, and based on the shape it was assumed – wrongly – most Elizabethan theatres adopted.

Sam Wanamaker's extraordinary campaign over years was another inspiration and his project to 'rebuild ' the Globe was coming to fruition. Sometime in the mid-nineties, several years after the creation of Kingston Theatre Trust (KTT) and after our work had been stalled by a recession, we appointed as theatre consultant Michael Holden who had contributed to the Globe project and had also for a time been its Chief Executive. My first conversation with him led easily to an idea for a modern theatre based on the original Rose. As a result Holden supervised an initial design inspired by the discovered archaeology. Some years later, when Peter Hall saw a more developed version of it he 'couldn't believe the audacity of the vision'.

This was not a romantic adventure in historical reproduction, attractive though that might be as an idea. There was the inevitable question of finance, and if the original Rose had a capacity of fifteen hundred, it was reckoned that a modern version with almost the same dimensions would take upwards of a thousand. This theatre would have to be able to 'wash its face' – as the euphemism for economic viability had it – and so potential capacity and, more importantly, average houses, were always important issues. Amongst the many answers to that question of why we built the Rose, the first and foremost one to many of those pushing the project forwards was a practical one: it was potentially economical, however slippery that word might mean in the context of any theatre project. That was probably the same argument that Philip Henslowe would have given in the late sixteenth century.

The question of what 'viability' means is complex, but for most it means simply the making of profit, or at least 'balancing the books'. When Colin Chambers, a long time associate of the Royal Shakespeare Company and author of the most authoritative history of that great company, asked me some years ago how things were going, I told him, 'There's a bit of a financial crisis at the moment'. His response was that, yes, of course there was: he knew of few theatres which were not in financial crisis. What his question meant was how was the work shaping up, how were the personnel settling, what was the repertoire looking like? Well, Henslowe became a very rich man and Edward Alleyn founded the 'College of God's Gift' – Dulwich College – but there was no great confidence that financial well-being, let alone auspicious guidance from above, would journey across the centuries.

Who were the players in this long stage saga? The company grew as the project developed of course. Some of the original principals did not remain to the fore, others fell by the wayside, but a hard core saw the project to opening. In the early days, it was a few renegades, vagabonds on the fringes – upstarts suggesting they knew what Kingston needed – who dominated the story. But soon the centre stage was taken by the indefinable Kingston, in its many guises: woman and man on the street, ratepayer, employer and employee, teacher and student. The other group of players which quickly joined came from the Royal Borough of Kingston, an institution of councillors and officers who, for one reason or another, became engaged or found themselves, sometimes unwittingly, implicated. At some point the University joined in; it existed in another form – Kingston Polytechnic – when the play started, and initially appeared indifferent. But there came a time – after 1992 and its transformation into Kingston University – when it wanted a bit of the action and so it played its part, graduating quickly, after a very short apprenticeship, to becoming a principal, and a most effective one at that.

This play was no brief 'two hours traffic of our stage'. It took a long time – years longer than some of us might have thought when the action began. But *had* it happened quickly, it would not have blossomed as it did: when the campaign to build a theatre in Kingston began, the extraordinary archaeological find on the Southbank was something for the future. As *The Sunday Times* said on the eve of the eventual opening, 'As improbable outcomes go, beat this: an unpromising commercial development in Kingston, southwest London, just happens to contain a near-perfect auditorium based on the plan of the Elizabethan Rose theatre'. This was in the context of an interview with Peter Hall, who was putting the finishing touches to *Uncle Vanya*, and he had said: 'It's to do with the English ability to make things happen by improvisation and informality. Who'd have thought that a copy of Shakespeare's Rose in modern guise would be built in Kingston because a group of Kingstonians wanted it? If someone had told you that, you'd have said, "It'll never happen"'.

2
Before the Rose

Theatres have played their role in Kingston's life and history for decades. As the Victorian age dwindled to its conclusion the Royal County Theatre opened in Fife Road on the 4th October 1897. It was a conversion from the Albany Assembly Rooms whose sister, the Surbiton Assembly Rooms, was to have a footnote in the story of the Rose. The Royal County was a house of variety, with plays, opera and pantomimes: the four-year-old Noel Coward saw his first pantomime, *Aladdin*, there in 1903. At the end of the Edwardian era, in 1912, its playing days appeared to be over and it converted itself in order to cash in on the new rage – moving pictures. It made intermittent attempts to discover its old theatrical identity before finally succumbing to fire in 1940.

The Empire Theatre was built on Clarence Street in 1910, sharing a birth date with some illustrious survivors – the New Theatre Royal, Windsor, the Wimbledon Theatre and the London Palladium. The building still stands opposite the 'Tumbling Telephone Boxes' sculpture at the junction with the Old London Road. The Empire had its brush with fire in 1919 when the auditorium was gutted, but it recovered to live on until television did for it: it finally gave up its ghosts in 1956, all but its name, the last vestiges of which can – just – be seen in the lettering "EMPIRE" as you approach Clarence Street from the south, along Fairfield West. For many years the name was fading to a trace, but recently it was renovated, only to be partially obscured again by an ugly brick elevation to the shop buildings in front.

In *The Book of Kingston* (1995), Shaan Butters writes 'Kingston has not had a proper theatre since the closure of the Empire'. This was not strictly

7

true: a Scotsman, Alan Bryce, and his wife began the Overground Theatre Club in 1974. Its first base was the Kingston Hotel and when that was demolished it moved into the All Saints Church Hall in Ashdown Road and gained some notice producing, in Bryce's words, 'anything and everything worth doing'. Many still have fond memories of the Overground although the work was of mixed quality. Bryce himself sometimes lacked sensitivity and was not always strategically astute: when he believed the Overground had lost out to London's Half Moon in gaining an Arts Council grant he is said to have responded rather meanly, 'It has only ten more seats than we have so why can't it be run more economically'. It chimes with my one contact with him, when I asked him if he might consider giving students reductions on ticket prices as there were no concessions and such a move would boost audience numbers. Bryce's response was a very blunt negative, which was calculated neither to encourage young theatre-goers nor boost ticket sales. In the Overground file at the V&A archive there is an Arts Council note in June 1979 for the Review Committee: 'An enterprising enterprise (*sic*) that perhaps looks too much for quantity as opposed to quality'. With the proposals to develop the Wheatfield Way, which was to provide relief to Kingston's centre from road traffic, a compulsory purchase order was made for the Overground building. Negotiations between the Royal Borough of Kingston (RBK), the Arts Council and Bryce fell down and he departed to the United States, from whence, a few years ago, he attributed the Overground's demise rather grandly to 'cuts made by the then-Prime Minister Margaret Thatcher'.

There is another trace of theatrical aspiration in the 1970s. Rowan Bentall, then Head of the Bentall dynasty, was involved with the formation of the Kingston Arts Trusts in 1976, with – amongst other things – the intention of building a theatre on the old boatyard site at Hampton Wick. Nothing came of this: twenty years later someone recalled that the Trusts were ostensibly still in existence and they were formally wound up.

Kingston at this time could demonstrate high class performance work in one field. When I arrived in Kingston in 1973 the town had something of a soul in its vibrant All Saints Church, the parish church which had a reputation for its choral work. The organist and irrepressible musical entrepreneur was David Nield. In 1977 the BBC Christmas Day Service was broadcast nationwide from Kingston, and in 1983 it was the turn of the Good Friday Service. Dissatisfied with an organ originally installed in Victorian times and adapted with varying degrees of success thereafter, Nield announced the need for a new organ. This would not be a sort of like-for-like replacement of its clapped-out nineteenth century instrument. Nield, a former organ scholar at Durham University, had ambition: the Parish Church would have a great organ and he took himself off to Denmark to the renowned firm of organ builders, Theodor Frobenius & Sons. The campaign attracted national interest and its very own BBC *Omnibus* documentary as well as the patronage of organists throughout the world, including the extraordinary Carlo Curley. The new organ was installed, a magnificent instrument for posterity and launched by a concert – with Curley at the console – in April 1986. Several recessions and collapsing pounds later, the debt on the invoice was finally paid, but in the meantime Kingston's soul was nourished and an example had been given of aiming high to fulfill an aspiration.

Even so, there was something lacking. The Overground had not been quite the answer to the cultural gap, nor could or should the church act as a substitute. Worse still, there were those for whom 'culture' meant 'Royal' Kingston, derived from the dubious historical image of lines of Saxon kings queuing up to be crowned in the market place or wherever the 'Coronation Stone' happened to be sited between 900 and 979 AD; with this throning stone, now so visible in front of the Guildhall, Kingston could sit back smugly and feel culturally replete. Today the official Royal Borough of Kingston website chooses its words carefully: thus, of the Coronation Stone, resuscitated from obscurity by our Victorian forebears, 'it is *traditionally* thought to have been used for the Coronation of *up to seven* Saxon Kings in the tenth century'. (The italics are mine). The historical association with royalty if a little over-egged is, however, no myth: the name Kingston is derived from 'cyninges tun' and means 'royal manor'. It is first found in a defence agreement between King Egbert and Coelnoth, Archbishop of Canterbury, at a council held at Kingston in 838. Coelnoth was buying the protection of Egbert against Viking raids. The Anglo-Saxon Chronicles record that King Athelstan was consecrated there. Doomsday Book records that Kingston was part of King Edward the Confessor's farm and that, with perhaps a whimsical association with the Sermon on the Mount, 'there was there a church, five mills and three fisheries'.

Royal associations have ricocheted down the years. A century and a half later, King John gave Kingston a Royal Charter in 1200. He was finally thanked in May 2016 with Trevor Nunn's production of Shakespeare's *King John* in the Rose Theatre. In 1603 James 1, even as he trekked slowly south from Edinburgh towards the plague-ravaged capital of his new kingdom, he made Shakespeare a Groom of his Chamber and granted Kingston a Saturday Market. A feature of the market place today is a gilded statue of Queen Anne. King George V confirmed Kingston's status as a Royal Borough in 1927 and in 1965, Queen Elizabeth 11 aced his king by granting another Royal Charter which entitles Kingston to continue to use the title 'Royal Borough of Kingston upon Thames'.

Even with the assurance that two and possibly three Saxon leaders were in fact consecrated under the watchful eye of their wandering entourages on the banks of the Thames, twentieth century Kingston ought, nevertheless, to have other exciting stories to tell from a rich national culture and, as importantly, a place in which to tell them. So we needed a theatre: that was our thinking, anyway!

3
A Commitment to Campaign

For Robin Hutchinson and me, the call to arms came first when Bonner Hill School, then situated at the bottom of Villiers Road, was closed in 1980. The school was encircled with a seven foot high whicker barrier and a threat against anyone attempting to trespass. The threat was as good as a goad and we determined that here was a site as practical as any on which to stage our stand for a theatre. Climbing the hoarding and balancing precariously on top, we announced the creation of what we called the Arts for Kingston campaign. A local reporter wrote that the campaigners wanted 'a commercial and educational theatre'. Demonstrating a degree of political naivety, we asked that anyone interested in supporting the campaign should contact me at my address. Although teaching in Kingston, I lived in Long Ditton and my house, one of a little row of cottages in Howard Street, was little more than a hundred yards *outside* the Royal Borough boundary. The response of one councillor, the Reverend Michael Mannell, was delightedly acerbic: he dismissed as impertinent the attempts of an organisation based outside the borough attempting to influence what happened within. As our campaign developed, this future Mayor of Kingston was triumphantly to declare himself and Kingston to be 'philistine and proud of it'.

Alongside our naivety we had also a youthfully challenging and pugnacious attitude: the local hack on the *Kingston Informer* seemed pleased to report that we were attacking the local Council's 'appalling record' in 'a strongly worded letter' sent – alas, for our short term local and political credibility – from my Long Ditton fastness. We were a 'newly formed group of residents who deplore the lack of support for the arts' and Kingston was 'culturally barren'. In what, in retrospect, were the seeds of his first speech as the councillor he had not yet become, Hutchinson is quoted as saying, 'Perhaps it is time the ratepayers were given the chance to be proud of their council rather than saddened at its neglect. While we have a council that has members who are proud to go on record as being philistines towards the arts there is little hope of change unless the community can convince those in power that they are not representing the wishes of the majority'. And thus the idea of a new theatre began to move into the mainstream of local issues.

It was not an especially promising time to be suggesting a new theatre, especially if it imagined drawing support from public funding. Little did I realize at the time how the next three decades would bring engagement with theatre finance, difficult then, but in many ways made more complex through the nineteen eighties. The Thatcher government had been in office for little over a year, when the notorious 'Christmas Cuts' of 1980 were announced by the Arts Council. From April the following year eighteen theatre companies were to have their grants withdrawn. The two decades since the appointment of Jennie Lee as the first ever Minister for the Arts, which had brought evident political approval and such positive developments, seemed a lifetime away: the arts now feared winters of discontent.

Despite this, theatrical activity – as it always will – continued to re-invent itself on national stages and in the regions. South of St.Austell in Cornwall another local teacher began to run some workshops in his spare time and soon all sorts of people from the local community became involved: 'a farmer, the sign writer from Tesco, several students, a thrash guitarist from a local band, an electrician ...' runs the historical note about Kneehigh, founded in 1980 by Mike Shepherd. For forty years Kneehigh delighted audiences with its unique invention, touring the world and winning awards, including Tony nominations on Broadway – until its sudden, shocking and saddening demise in June 2021, at another difficult moment for theatre.

At the National, meanwhile, Michael Bogdanov was directing Howard Brenton's *The Romans in Britain*, with its brilliant critique of imperialism dramatised most notably if not as graphically as some asserted, in the scene depicting the attempted homosexual rape of a tribesman by a Roman centurion. It seems as pertinent today as it did four decades ago, but

Horace Cutler, then the leader of the Greater London Council, suggested the grant to the National should be cut, while Mary Whitehouse – who never saw the production – brought a private prosecution which hung over Bogdanov for the next two years. The National's Artistic Director, Peter Hall, was at work on his landmark *Oresteia*, in a new translation by Tony Harrison with music by Harrison Birtwhistle, while his friend and former protégé Trevor Nunn was collaborating for the first time with composer Andrew Lloyd Webber and producer Cameron Mackintosh on a dramatisation of T.S.Eliot's *Old Possum's Book of Practical* Cats; in May 1981 *Cats* opened at the New London Theatre. The following year, *Top Girls* would have its premiere at the Royal Court, Richard Eyre's *Guys and Dolls* would open at the National and a small group of visionaries, influenced by Jacques Lecoq in Paris, would quietly launch Théâtre de Complicité, now known simply as Complicité. Despite the funding gloom, the first couple of years of the new decade had some distinctive high points.

Our Bonner Hill demonstration was by no means my first venture with Robin Hutchinson. When I arrived in Kingston in 1973 to teach at Tiffin School he was one of my students. He had played a passable Polonius and a vocally assured, if somewhat warrior-slight, Hotspur in early productions I directed. He really came into his own as a gloriously irresponsible Toad, in *Toad of Toad Hall*, which I did not direct. His real skill lay in brilliant improvisation and invention, as attested by his later career and his standing in Kingston now. He always found it difficult to learn someone else's words or sing from another's song-sheet. By the time he left school to go to Chelsea School of Art we had become firm friends and enjoyed nothing more than creating a variety of performance work, which we played in school halls, pubs, clubs and on barges. A Lancastrian by birth, Hutchinson had been in Kingston from an early age, when his father became Director of Social Services for Merton Council in the early seventies. No model student, school nevertheless whetted Hutchinson's appetite for questioning all that came his way, especially if it was 'authority' or self-satisfied convention. He made his mark, but his mark was neither then, nor subsequently, always to everyone's taste. He had strong views and, in his early days, could deliver these with a certain abrasiveness which, as he matured, developed into articulate argument with a razor-sharp wit.

His instincts were and are fundamentally populist: nothing thrills him more than mobilising people on projects which are or might become important in their everyday lives. He does this in ways which are often extraordinary or extravagant, but almost always which have some idiosyncratic logic. His long flowing locks, his reputation as *the* local rock singer, known affectionately as Screaming Lord Hutch (his group, *The Reptiles*, performs to this day, invariably in the interests of a range of charities) and his ability to engage in controversial argument on a range of community issues made him, and makes him, a natural honey pot for local media attention. He made friends and enemies with equal ease, although he is now more tempered. He became increasingly politically astute and articulate, qualities which – alongside his intellectual strengths – were not always readily recognised.

Others were wary of him, even after he became a founding member of the Theatre Trust: the Trust should after all, they believed, be a group made up of local worthies. On one occasion years later, I was leaving a meeting in the Guildhall and a fellow trustee on the Kingston Theatre Trust and occasional attendee of the meetings, a local 'worthy' from Kingston Hill, was heard to say, 'You know, that Robin Hutchinson is cleverer than you might think'. I had thought and did know, so I merely smiled that it had taken this person nearly two decades to realise. Without Robin, I think Kingston would not now have a theatre.

Our Arts for Kingston campaign needed to maintain a momentum and also needed some political credibility. Simply creating publicity opportunities would not sustain and develop it. However, we found there was already a potential, if somewhat diffuse, support base. There were those who were saddened at the demise of the Overground; there were others who still remembered the Empire; and there was a growing number, many of them quite young, who wanted Kingston to become culturally more exciting.

Nationally, the debate about arts development and funding was about to be injected with new life with the 1984 Arts Council review, *The Glory of the Garden*. This highlighted the discrepancy between theatre and the arts in London and the situation in the regions. Especially since the building of the M25, Kingston found itself in an ambiguous position, attached as it had become to the capital by virtue of a concrete necklace. At this time certainly Robin Hutchinson and I were campaigning for a theatre which would give Kingston a sense of identity. As Kate Dorney and Ros Merkin were later to reflect in a substantial book reviewing *The Glory of the Garden* and the years which followed, such theatres gave, 'a sense of who we are in all its complexities and contradictions, a sense of our Community'.

We did not anticipate at this time that our theatre should enhance the London scene. Nor did we particularly engage in a philosophical discussion about what theatre should be doing: should it reflect creative excellence – a Keynesian ideal – or should it be more about access to theatre entertainment for the greatest number?

The Villiers Road site which we had attempted to lay claim to soon disappeared to a private housing developer, but another intriguing and more central opportunity began to emerge: the so called 'Power Station site'. Kingston's first power station was built close to Canbury Gardens in 1893. Its access to the river was its value: the coal which fired it was transported by barge up the Thames and the water which cooled it came from the same source. When the power station was finally decommissioned in 1980, initial planning proposals were for office development and later there was a shift towards housing and some 'recreation'. We happily seized upon the potential this offered and for a while in the mid-eighties it became the adopted site for the theatre. Irrespective of the huge problems associated with removing quantities of asbestos, or almost because of them, a theatre was the answer. As with so many leftover units of industrial England, here was the site for cultural regeneration. Council officers even began to consider the possibility, including the suggestion of a theatre auditorium alongside a hotel in an evolving planning brief. Whilst the Council could not specify to the owners, the Central Electricity Generating Board, what it should put on its site, RBK would have to grant planning permission, and so a 'planning brief' acted as a guide to what might be acceptable. In the end the focus moved elsewhere, but the idea of making something useful out of something redundant certainly sustained and developed the theatre cause for a while and added public interest and support.

In the meantime, it was evident that we would need to find other new individual impetuses and to give ourselves new strengths in order to move things forward. As far as Robin Hutchinson was concerned, this was calculated: he went into local politics. For my part, my developing expertise was incidental. For over a decade I had been directing a variety of productions every year with young people, including a large number of Shakespeare's plays, but now my theatre experience was about to expand. I was also lucky that one of my colleagues at Tiffin School was David Nield. What was to happen over the next few years gave me a voice of some small sort as the movement to build a theatre in Kingston grew.

Music at Tiffin School was flourishing under Nield. In late 1984 he was commissioned to compose a work for the Shaftesbury Society to celebrate the centenary of the death of its founder, Anthony Ashley Cooper, the seventh Earl of Shaftesbury. Shaftesbury's place in history rests on his extraordinary work as a social reformer and his particular concern was the exploitation of children. David asked me to write the lyrics of what would become *Six Songs for a Ragged School Child*. This inevitably meant a great deal of research into social conditions in Victorian London and also some exciting Drama workshops with some of my young students. In the event many of the final lyrics came from two of my collaborators, the twelve year old twins, Ian and Paul McLachlan, with Nield's musical composition. The work was presented at the Shaftesbury Centenary Concert at the Queen Elizabeth Hall on the South Bank in 1985, with the Tiffin Choir and the National Youth Orchestra. Amongst other performers that night, the glorious Evelyn Glennie played percussion and Richard Stilgoe was the compère.

Even before the event it was evident that the material offered opportunities for a serious piece of music theatre. So David and I joined forces with Jeremy James Taylor and we wrote a ballad opera called *The Ragged Child*. Taylor had been an associate director with the brilliant Young Vic company in the seventies, under first Frank Dunlop and then Michael Bogdanov. His interest in musical theatre led him to create an organisation called the Children's Music Theatre and a number of schools benefitted from a collaboration with him. With David Nield's inspiration, several light jazz musicals were made and performed at Tiffin School and elsewhere. The work extended into ballad operas and musicals and embraced schools across the country and involved an annual two or three weeks on the Edinburgh Fringe. Professional producers began to take an interest and the CMT became the National Youth Music Theatre, with the approval of Peter Hall and of Trevor Nunn, the artistic directors of the two leading national companies. Michael Croft, the founder and director of the National Youth Theatre, who might have opposed the name change, forgot to reply to our letter asking if he objected until after the first successful Edinburgh season under the new NYMT banner in 1985.

In March 1986 *The Ragged Child* was performed at Tiffin School. Within weeks we re-wrote and re-rehearsed it as a National Youth Music Theatre production. Amongst a talented young cast, were the thirteen years old Jonny Lee Miller and the sixteen years old Jo Davies, who would be appointed in 2023 as the first female artistic director of Opera Australia at the Sydney Opera House. In June we took it to the Bergen Festival in Norway, to Den Nationale Scene, Ibsen's theatre. We were to play on the Edinburgh Fringe, but Frank Dunlop, newly appointed Director of the International Festival and desiring more theatre in that year's repertoire, invited us onto the International programme. To be a part of the Edinburgh International Festival brought great kudos to the young NYMT. *The Ragged Child* had an extraordinary impact, fêted by the national press, and with much television coverage for three weeks morning, noon and night. It was the early days of breakfast television, which we delightedly exploited. The George Square theatre sold out for performance after performance. There was a Royal Gala performance, attended by the young Prince Edward, who would shortly become the President of the NYMT, a post he holds to this day, as the Duke of Edinburgh. He is also now the very active President of the charity Creative Youth, organisers of Fuse International, formerly the International Youth Arts Festival, held at the Rose Theatre annually – and so Kingston's royal connection is maintained.

For me as a writer and director of the piece, it both fuelled and confirmed a number of convictions and led to opportunities to direct work with young people on a number of major stages around the world in the years to come. As the NYMT began to have invitations to theatres both in Britain and abroad, I harboured the ambition that at some time productions like this would come to a theatre in Kingston and I took every opportunity to talk about the importance of Kingston having such a theatre. Over two decades later, I was pleased that *The Ragged Child* was one of the first productions in the inaugural season of the Rose in 2008 and that the NYMT has been so central to the development and success of Kingston's Fuse International.

For his part, meanwhile, in the late nineteen eighties, Robin Hutchinson had become actively engaged in local politics. The political dimension was to be one of the most important aspects in the creation of Kingston's theatre, and in some respects a distinctive example for local authorities throughout the country. Hutchinson abandoned the Liberal Party connections which he had had, albeit fairly loosely, up until that time and he was adopted as the prospective Labour Councillor for Tolworth West. It was an interesting move, given that the Labour Party in Kingston seemed likely always to play second fiddle to the Liberal Party as opposition to the Conservatives, the perennial party in power. Robin was a colourful addition to the local Labour cause. Brian Willman, many years later a Kingston Theatre Trustee, was then a prospective Labour candidate for the Council. He recalls that at candidate meetings, 'the dominant voice was Robin's with a stream of ideas for policies and tactics, with his sense of humour used to great effect'. It was during these meetings that the promotion of better arts provision in the Borough came to the fore and the question of a theatre moved into the political mainstream. Hutchinson took every opportunity for publicity: in the early days of Channel Four, he appeared on its 'Comment' slot to berate Kingston's ruling group for its 'shallow and ill-considered' arts policy. Blunt, even when mixing metaphors, he picked up on an earlier Tory attack on the Arts for Kingston campaign: 'Kingston Council, with its head-in-the-ground philistine attitude, has missed the boat completely on GLC funding for arts facilities'. The Conservative's Chairman of the Arts and Recreation Committee, one Trevor Thorpe, countered that he was considering setting up a trust to investigate the building of an 'arts centre': 'We even considered it before Mr. Hutchinson went on television', he said, before adding rather lamely that he was not aware of the possibility of GLC funding.

The theatre (or 'arts centre' – the discrepancy in the reference would inevitably cause controversy later) was now the subject of political debate. As the local elections of May 1986 approached the Liberals too were beginning to develop an arts argument: it was a prominent feature in their 12-point manifesto. Roger Hayes, another future theatre trustee, was Liberal Party Councillor in Canbury ward and the prospective Parliamentary candidate for his party. He said, 'The prime site for a theatre must be the power station site'.

At national level, politics had a distinctive flavour, if some were left with a nasty taste in their mouths: the Tory government under Margaret Thatcher had polarised attitudes. Following a breakaway from the Labour Party, the 'Gang of Four' – Shirley Williams, Bill Rodgers, David Owen and Roy Jenkins – had formed the SDP and had gone into a loose partnership known as 'the Alliance' with the Liberal Party, led by David Steel. It would be a further two years before they formally merged as the Liberal Democrats, leaving Owen to his own devices. Meanwhile, the Labour Party was struggling to come to terms with the SDP split and with the mauling it had received at the 1983 General Election.

The political colour of Kingston, perennially blue, did not entirely reflect the nation: there was going to be a dramatic shift, although initially neither decisively nor permanently. But the days of Kingston as a Conservative fiefdom were over, even though another decade would pass before Ed Davey shook the mould at parliamentary level. On the 8th May 1986, all the seats were up for election on Kingston's council. The people of the Royal Borough delivered a shock: no party had over-all control. The Labour group of four, which included the newly-elected Councillor Robin Hutchinson, joined the Liberal/SDP Alliance to enable an administration to form.

There was fervent activity. Kingston's Liberals were largely of the 'Young' type – the heirs of the thrusting, vibrant and contentious Young Liberal movement of the late sixties and seventies, most notorious when Peter Hain was their Chairman. They had a reforming zeal and moved swiftly into action, not least to attempt the reform of education in the Borough, one of the remaining authorities with selective grammar and secondary modern schools. To move so quickly on this was a political misjudgment and would prove their temporary nemesis in a few short months. In the meantime, Hutchinson matched the Liberals in his zeal by proposing the potentially contentious motion in the first full Council meeting, seconded by his colleague Phil Cooper, that a theatre should be built. This elicited the first round of tutting from traditionalists: the first full Council meeting after elections should have been preserved for non-political 'mayor-making' activity, not acting as a stage to place the establishment of a theatre at the top of the political agenda!

Within a week of the elections, at the first Planning Committee meeting, Cooper proposed that the next planning brief should include a theatre provision on the power station site. The new committee chairman was Roger Hayes and he backed the plan. In the glare of the headlights, the Tories dithered: Tony Martin said, 'I don't subscribe to the view that every town should have a theatre'. They had not yet grasped the fact that it was now becoming a popular option, nor that they might be seen – not least, in the light of recent statements by the Conservative Trevor Thorpe – as trying to ride one horse in opposite directions at the same time.

There was activity outside the Guildhall. As I was about to depart to Edinburgh for the 1986 Festival I had a moment of déjà vu: there was an announcement of the creation of a new arts group, designed to keep the pressure on the politicians to deliver an arts centre: it was to be called Arts for Kingston!

4
Like to a Double Cherry...

That there were two Arts for Kingston organisations – let alone the already dormant Kingston Arts Trusts – was not the only sign of a need for forces to co-ordinate. The question of where to build the theatre seemed to have been settled in the local press with the power station site creating so much attention. However, there were other possibilities, not least Charter Quay, even closer to the centre of Kingston, emerging from the mists of a medieval past and now considered ripe for development. The most important discrepancy to resolve was over what sort of theatre would be built. Should it be a theatre, used principally for the presentation of plays, or should it be an arts centre, a multi-purpose space? There were already signs of a divergence of opinion and a polarisation of views. The two are not necessarily mutually exclusive, but rarely does the building of one multi-purpose space satisfy the demands of specialist practitioners, whether in drama, music or dance, let alone other art forms and film shows. With huge national investment in a number of different spaces within one building – such as Washington's Kennedy Center, with a variety of specialised spaces, or the Sydney Opera House, with its opera space and separate theatre space – diversity of intention can work, but Kingston had no such grand pretension. In this country, the Derngate Centre in Northampton was built in the 1980s, but not until 2005 when it underwent an expensive renovation and amalgamation with the nineteenth century Theatre Royal and with the addition of a cinema did it really begin to satisfy diverse needs, as the Royal and Derngate.

The rhetoric had certainly, in the years leading up to the 1986 local elections, characterised Kingston as a cultural wasteland. Robin

Hutchinson and I had had from the outset the idea that it was a theatre which was first and foremost needed to replenish the town. This was reflected in the political responses of all the parties who referred to 'a theatre'. In my mind, I envisaged a working theatre with a company of actors and an artistic director. Robin and I often talked about a theatre which would have not only an impact on Kingston and its close environs, but one which would have regional, even national impact for the distinctive quality of its work. However, at this stage our thoughts were general: other than asserting that the work would be excellent, we defined 'distinctive' no further for the time being.

The *new* Arts for Kingston campaign, on the other hand, was intent on building 'an arts centre'. This popular pressure group was led by Brian Willman, apparently oblivious to the existence of that movement of the same name created by Robin Hutchinson and me. It says more about our failure to sustain ours as an organisation in the public eye than does it indicate myopia on Willman's part: we had remained as mavericks, looking for publicity opportunities, garnering support, but not establishing an organisation on the ground which people could sign up to and identify with. Brian Willman had, following an inaugural meeting at the Druid's Head in late June 1986, quickly developed a strong support base of individuals and local groups and thus there was a membership identity. Vicky Wilding had become chairperson and Willman had also enlisted the support of the eccentric local actor Ron Forfar and the Musicians' Union national organiser, Maurice Jennings. The actress Julia McKenzie became Honorary President: Willman says now, 'I have no idea how we got in touch with her. She lived near me in Canbury and I suspect I pushed a note through her door and she wrote back. I don't remember ever meeting her'. So even the new kid on the block was a bit haphazard!

Julia McKenzie had been the definitive Miss Adelaide in the recent *Guys and Dolls*, a production so successful it transferred in 1985 to the West End from the Southbank, whilst the RSC opened a musical production of Victor Hugo's *Les Miserables* at their London Barbican base. Peter Hall, still at the National, had recently directed Ian McKellen in *Coriolanus* and had given the go-ahead to the production of a brilliant new play probing the press, *Pravda* by David Hare and Howard Brenton.

Back in Kingston, the stated objective of Willman's Arts for Kingston campaign was for arts facilities, and most particularly an arts centre, on the power station site. There were frequent meetings and in September an event, known as AFK Day, was held in Kingston Market Place. It was notable for the attention it received: the third newsletter reported, 'the combination of sun, jazz and clowns was a perfect cocktail'. Four thousand leaflets were distributed and over two hundred people returned slips indicating approval. The Kingston Polytechnic Students' Union also gave support. Windows around the town began to display the AFK logo with 'I support a Kingston Arts Centre'. The AFK Day on the 27th September 1986 was more than a celebration of the emergence of an effective pressure group; it was an important contribution to help shape the public response to a consultation on arts provision which took place a few months later.

AFK had won the support of some twenty local societies as well as numerous individuals. By the following January, it boasted five hundred members. Brian Willman, by now its secretary, was reported as saying that, 'An arts centre would give identity to all of Kingston's cultural groups, providing them with much-needed facilities and a central arena for performance'. In the second AFK newsletter, published in August, there was a clearer statement of aims and objectives which included six points, the first four of which made an explicit commitment to 'an Arts Centre'. The following January, Wilding and Willman declared 1987 'The Year of the Arts Centre'.

As time progressed, we would have to ensure that everyone knew exactly what sort of facility they were campaigning for. Should this become a bone of contention it might damage any political commitment. Whilst a rose by any other name would smell as sweet, 'arts centre' is not a synonym for 'theatre' and vice versa, whatever features they might have in common. A political initiative took place which should have helped in this: the RBK Arts and Recreation committee determined at its first post-election meeting in 1986 that a working party should be set up to look into the provision of arts facilities in the centre of Kingston. The Working Party, which came together in the Autumn, comprised councillors, council officers and others, amongst whom were Brian Willman and me. The Working Party was chaired by John McCarthy, who was the Chairman of the Kingston Arts Council. We were to consider what existed at the moment and to propose potential developments. We quickly determined that there was not a great deal to detain us in the first task and so we divided into three sub-groups to examine potential developments: an arts centre or theatre; a library; a large music hall with a conference centre.

I joined the first sub-group, looking at the arts centre/ theatre idea, a group which Brian Willman chaired. Willman was now the leading spokesman for AFK, which was determined to build an arts centre. Whilst I would have been pleased should we achieve this as an outcome, it was not my aim: I cherished the dream of a professional theatre. We had very frank discussions and it was evident that there were some quite divergent aspirations. There was also a concern from some that we should be 'realistic', which was sensible enough, but not necessarily a premise for innovative, original and imaginative thinking. It is clear when reading our report in retrospect that we were intent on maintaining a momentum towards establishing a building, without having fully resolved its character and the philosophical thrust: it would be an 'arts centre' which would have as its principal feature a 'theatre/performance area'; it would meet the 'demands of local societies as well as professional theatre'; the acoustic qualities 'should be biased towards the spoken word' whilst being 'also suitable for music performance'; 'sufficient land is required for a building [of] approximately 3,100 sq. metres'; there would be a 'studio/rehearsal room approximately 30' x 30'. Some might characterise this group as open-minded, others might say we sat uncomfortably on the fence, whilst others still might think that there were diplomatic tactics in evidence, but as yet there was no clear strategy from any direction.

Whilst we specified the dimension of a studio (which is more or less the size of the current Rose Studio, and which happened to be the size of a studio I was then building at Tiffin School) we made no such stipulation about the 'theatre' other than suggesting a capacity of 'around 400'. It might have been that some assumed a proscenium theatre, others an 'end on' with courtyard features: certainly, the Wilde Centre in Bracknell became a reference point, and we had a committee outing there. It was important that we were not driven into any particular *cul de sac*, and in our section on finance it was clearly stated that, 'The costs [should] not reflect any particular form of planning or construction but can be considered to cover a wide range of forms and construction of arts centres'.

The balancing act was clear in our management proposals: this must both respond to 'the needs of the local societies' and 'the needs of professional theatre, such as touring companies ... (it is considered the provision of a full time professional theatre in the town centre is desirable but not of the highest priority)'. The very phrasing in the parenthesis suggests some of us placed the priority higher than others, but we did not want to fall out at this stage!

One important change in focus was on where any facility might be built: as far as a site was concerned we turned our attention to places other than the power station, focusing especially on Emms Boatyard, which was a part of the Charter Quay and a rather run-down area, much closer to the centre of Kingston. The report also considered the near derelict Ashdown Road area and the so-called 'Heritage site', which included the Library and its Grade II listed façade. This latter consideration assumed the relocation of the Library. We were clear there were no other options.

In a section on management the seeds of the Kingston Theatre Trust were sown: 'Responsibility for management ... could be through a self governing body which would then achieve its functions without direct local authority control ... [It] would rely heavily on revenue contribution from the local authority to meet overall costs'. Preliminary estimates of basic building costs indicated Emms Boatyard would be £3.33 million, the Heritage site, £2.67 million, Ashdown Road, £3.33 million and the Power Station, £3.58 million. We also suggested a programme which would allow for the building to be completed by the winter of 1991. Well, we did not manage that target: even the shell of the eventual theatre was to be over a decade late in arriving. But that does not look too bad when compared to other projects. There was a wait of nearly a century from the time a National Theatre was first mooted by the likes of William Archer and George Bernard Shaw in the late nineteenth century until its opening in 1976!

The two other sub-groups on the Working Party produced very different reports. The 'Large Hall Auditorium' report was little more than a bare outline document with some non-committal options. The 'Library' report, on the other hand, was concerned about the pressing need for change as the current provision was 'no longer capable of readily satisfying needs'. Even so, the Library had to wait until 2008 – the year the theatre finally opened – for the extensive renovation and refurbishment that it needed, and a few years more before Cameron's coalition tried to kill libraries off completely.

In April 1987, in the light of these reports, RBK ran a consultation exercise which received nearly 2300 responses, the vast majority of whom wanted Kingston to do better on the arts and over 50% of whom wanted 'an arts centre'. The Working Party report on the theatre/ arts centre proposal was seen as a planning brief and RBK quickly announced the £4 million provision for the building on the Emms' Boatyard section of Charter Quay, to open in 1991. It is interesting to look back at that financial commitment, in the context of arguments about the local authority's obligations in the years which followed. At the time there was a cross-party and near unanimous commitment to this capital investment.

Brian Willman announced a second AFK Day in the town centre for 24th October 1987 and shortly afterwards wound up the organisation. Willman recalls, 'We drank a toast and went home feeling we had served a purpose and there was nothing more to do'. Perhaps that was a little naïve. However, although it would be twenty one years more before the official opening of the Rose, the Arts for Kingston campaign had achieved a number of very important things: a popular movement for the arts had gathered five hundred members within six months of its creation (or re-creation, whichever way you look at it: but, while Robin Hutchinson and I had attracted vocal support and got the political wheels turning, only he and I were ever 'members' in 1982). Willman quite rightly says that the response to AFK was 'an early predictor of the success of the Rose Friends'. He is also right in his reflection on the breadth of support: 'We were popular by being all things to all people. Among our supporters were Kingston Operatic Society, the adult learning WEA New Malden, and Cantati Camerati. Given that the Musicians' Union and full time actors were also involved, there was potential for major bust-ups if we ever got involved in detail'.

There would be residual tensions: the idea that the theatre in Kingston would become the venue in which local groups would perform their work was cherished by many as time went on, and certainly some felt that the final outcome was a betrayal of their aspirations. While the local authority used the 1987 Working Party 'Arts Centre' report as a planning brief, there were anomalies and hostages to fortune which would need to be resolved at a later date. Was it an example of effective strategic planning? No, of course it was not. However, a public need and aspiration had been exposed and a public interest stimulated which had, in turn, given rise to some political initiative. It was a start.

5
Chartering the Quay

Only a naïve would have believed that a commitment by the Council of the Royal Borough of Kingston to build a theatre would have led to the swift appearance of dramatic activity in a purpose-built space. The *bone fide* assurance of £4,000,000 in the capital budget might have been a confidence-booster early on, but as the years passed so too did elation and then expectation. Nearly a decade and a half later, when the aforementioned Brian Willman was invited to join the other furrowed brows on the Kingston Theatre Trust which presided over an as-yet-unfinished theatre, all were more hard-headed and realistic.

The Council's response in 1987 to the Working Party's proposals was swift and, it seemed, decisive: by August its Arts and Recreation Committee had endorsed the building of a space variously referred to as 'a theatre', 'an arts centre' and 'an arts facility'. This was ratified in full Council in late September. But the subsequent two decades saw a strange concatenation of events: there was 'stop-start' movement, moments of shrewd judgment, others of uncertain decision-making, cunning and connivance with frustration and optimism, all competing for position. As the years passed there was some detailed and careful planning, there was some strategic invention, there was some brilliant opportunism, there was serendipity and there was happenstance which resulted finally in an extraordinary theatre, but it was a long and winding road.

The Working Party proposals were, as I said, treated as planning briefs. A year later, at its meeting in September 1988, the Policy and Resources Committee of RBK approved the provision of £425,000, out of the capital allocation, to be spent in 1988/89 on 'preliminary works' towards the provision. The capital sum would be funded by deferred purchase arrangements, to realize £3 million and a further £1 million from the utilization of capital receipts. To me this commitment of nearly half a million was as good an assurance that the remainder would follow in due course as any certainty that raced. However, this £4 million was to become a significant factor in debates during the years to come, largely owing to its non-appearance, and the Council commitment increasingly resembled a limping nag. In the end, the money had no more substance than many another politician's promissory note.

A theatre consultant was recruited. For the first, though not the last time, RBK turned to Arts Business Limited. They were commissioned to study the proposal and to prepare a report, particularly on likely costs. ABL had access to anyone who would give them an opinion about what might be required. Both Robin Hutchinson and I found that we were frequently consulted by Alan Giddings of ABL as it seemed that we were seen as the local leaders on matters theatrical, roles we adopted without demur. A virtual theatre space was imagined from which some costs were developed along with an assessment of some sort of audience potential. What we did not immediately realise was that some of the very people who had engaged ABL had other priorities. Arts Business was employed by the Council and so it was to the Council and its officers that they were to answer.

Fluctuating political winds seemed to offer an interesting instability: the Conservatives had held the Council since time immemorial, but it was a coalition of the Liberals and Labour which had set up the 1986/87 Working Party. A year or so later, however, the Tories were back in the driving seat following a by-election in 1988 and they determined the next steps forward in terms of political decision-making. At this time, the theatre was clearly seen as a vote-winner, such was the public voice, and so plans began to move forwards initially with all-party support. There were waverers and there were those who would oppose the theatre, though as yet they were waiting in the wings, other than the self-professed philistine, the Reverend Mannell.

The Working Party had suggested four possible sites for a theatre/arts centre, but had steered the Council towards the Emms Boatyard site. Now, however, a striking opportunity arose which seemed to suggest fortune was on our side: Kingston was on the move with a commercial development which was to be a part of a town regeneration and for which a brief had been approved in April 1987. The idea was that a theatre would become a part of this plan for the riverside site, known as Charter Quay, which stretched effectively from Kingston Bridge southwards as far as Emms passage and eastwards to the Market place and High Street. The proximity of Old Father Thames was captivating: there was something Stratfordian in the idea. I heard no-one point out that river frontage hardly mattered to an audience in a darkened auditorium and those for whom the top priority was the development of culture and the arts found themselves at one with those who had inherited the Victorian motivation of the cultivation of civic pride. Some were surprised by their bedfellows, though no-one seemed to have awoken either with a hangover or a nasty rash - as yet.

The area under consideration was barely accessible, being made up as it was principally of old buildings, warehouses and yards dating back to Victorian times and farther. It was little better than a wasteland, yet it was on one of the most attractive and valuable stretches of the Thames. It also had history: it was named in recognition of the 1200 Royal Charter granted to Kingston by King John. A copy dated 1208 survives and it is this which has caused so many Kingston burghers over centuries to puff out their chests just a little further. Effectively, the Charter meant that the citizens of Kingston had some muscle: they had argued successfully that they should be allowed to by-pass the Sheriff in paying taxes. Prior to this, the Sheriff would act as a sort of tax-collecting middleman, setting his own fee into the bargain, so the Charter would, amongst other things, now thwart him. 'Our Freemen of Kingston' would be able forthwith to pay their dues directly to the King's Exchequer. That the figure now required was higher than that formerly expected was off-set by the reduction of bureaucratic corruption and the gain of honour and prestige in a more direct royal association.

The 'Quay' element related to trade by water. Commerce flourished in the thirteenth century, with the river and the market playing their part, notably in a wine trade with Gascony and a flourishing pottery

industry. Shaan Butters, in describing developments after the granting of
the Charter, writes of 'substantial late thirteenth century building' and
'contemporary building at Charter Quay' (*The Book of Kingston*, 1995).
Commercial prosperity and the markets were again to play their role
as Kingston strove for another significant development at the end of
the twentieth century. It had the potential to be one of the most transforming developments in Kingston's history, which inevitably meant that
there would be much debate, discussion and, inevitably at some points,
dissension.

The largest landowner on the site in the nineteen-eighties was the
Prudential – the 'solid as a rock' Pru – although we were unsure how
much our proposals would move them. The company announces proudly
today: 'Prudential was founded in London in 1848 on the principles of
integrity, security and prudence, and we still adhere to those values'.
There is a sense of assurance: 'We help to remove uncertainty from life's
big events, providing our customers with the freedom to face the future
with greater confidence'. A similar sense of security was given by the
other two major landowners, both with pedigree: F W Woolworth was
a global symbol of high street commercial success, founded in New York
in 1879 as 'Woolworth's Great Five Cent Store'; Friends Provident was
originally a Quaker foundation by Joseph Rowntree and Samuel Tuke in
Yorkshire in 1832. It was anticipated that neither would prove obstructive
to a development which would enhance the profit-making potential of
the town. This judgment was to prove misguided in the case of Friends
Provident, their Quaker non-conformism possibly getting the better
of their public-spirited altruism. Or perhaps their reticence was merely
pecuniary.

Meanwhile, elsewhere in Kingston, the new Bentall's Centre – a sort of
shopping mall – was making constructive headway. Bentall's was a name
inextricably associated with Kingston: it had been established in 1867
by Frank Bentall as a draper's shop and had thrived to become a large
department store. Even Woolworths had expressed an interest in moving
to the new Bentall's development. Construction had begun in 1987
and would take five years to complete. In the upshot dear old 'Woolies',
concealing clay feet, stayed put in the Market Place until its sudden and

shocking global expiration, an early victim of recession. Its demise was, ironically, only a few months after the Rose Theatre finally opened in 2008. In this game of riverside Monopoly, however, there was one crucial and fortuitous detail: RBK owned a small but significant part of the site and it was this which controlled access to the whole area and so would be an important levering tool in negotiations. It was our 'ransom plot'.

The Prudential and its architects, Building Design Partnership, moved quickly to produce plans for a mixture of town houses, flats, offices, shops and restaurants. Added excitement was that, as a 'planning gain', the Prudential would provide the *shell* of a theatre at its own cost. This detail would become the focus of much attention in the years to come. The shell of the theatre would be a part of Phase Two of the development. By May 1988 BDP put on public display, lasting a week, details of their plans, which even included impressions of 'the foyer of the proposed Charter Quay arts centre'. Whoever had been consulted – and it was no one who had been involved up until that time – and whoever had given expert advice, this exhibition strove to appear to be very impressive.

However – ungenerous and ungrateful though the thought may be – there came a sneaking feeling that we were being fobbed off. The good old Pru', founded in the nineteenth century as the paternal-sounding Widows and Orphans Friendly Society, was going to do rather well out of all this; and so, we felt, reciprocal arrangements should likewise do rather well for Kingston. The 'new theatre and arts centre', as it became known on Prudential documents, was there in the development, in amongst a proposed shopping arcade, but hidden away from both the Market Place and the riverside. I remember wondering if one would have as much difficulty finding it as punters did on visiting another important and recently opened theatre: in the five or six years since its inauguration, the Barbican Theatre in the City of London had given its resident the Royal Shakespeare Company a permanent corporate headache and an unknown number of their audience members, lost in an urban labyrinth, had simply failed to turn up for performances in one or other of its auditoria. Would you, we wondered, either find yourself in the Kingston 'theatre and arts centre' without realising you were there or, having bought a ticket, simply fail to show up? It was from this point that we determined that the theatre must have a street presence and its own welcoming entrance.

Brian Willman hastily re-formed Arts for Kingston and called to his mailing list that it was 'Time for your comments'! He proposed that 'a significant river frontage is dedicated to the Arts Centre and not merged ambiguously with commercial uses'. He further reflected on 'countless horror stories of arts centres built with faults that could have been foreseen'. Whether access from the water was at odds with presence on the streets was not yet debated. However, there was unanimity amongst the campaigners that submersion in some sort of mini metro-centre was not a good idea.

The local press was alert to the potential of controversy: in those days local papers were anything but the bland composites, functioning largely for the advertisers, as today's grey sheets are. In September 1988, the *Kingston Guardian* reporter was at a committee meeting in the Guildhall, which led to a delightful exercise in semantic extravagance: 'Seventy million pounds, secret talks behind closed doors and the future of Kingston at stake ... All the ingredients of a cracking good thriller, if not Shakespeare, were thrown into the script as the council's Development Committee meeting last week gave the thumbs up to a new arts centre for Kingston'. It went on that the Labour leader, Councillor Robin Hutchinson (his political ascension had been speedy) had in 'fiery speeches beforehand ... predicted that the 550-seat theatre and community arts complex would be a massive flop ... Hutchinson now seems destined for the role of the villain or spoiler of the piece by picking on council officers and seemingly trying to ruin Kingston's chances of gaining a theatre ... And in the best traditions of Victorian melodrama he has a black beard to help him play the part'!

Hutchinson, whilst always aware of theatrical possibility, was anything but the spoiling villain: his position was, in point of fact, perfectly reasonable. Proper consideration was not being given to the very particular needs that a theatre requires in order to be successful – and as far as he and I were concerned it was now to be a front-ranking theatre. Ever colourful in Council, he was drawing attention to the fact that a rigorous scrutiny of the plans was not taking place. Indeed, people were neither being consulted effectively nor was it possible to bring arguments to bear in order to make changes where poor decisions were being made. The cooking up of plans behind closed doors played out in various ways. This was to become a feature of the conduct of council officers for a number of years. Not until the practice ended did we finally move forward and build the theatre.

What was going on? With the Conservatives back in control, following the eighteen months interregnum, council officers seemed to have slipped easily back into the days of the old hegemony, where the idea of consultation was unheard of. It was like a local *Yes, Minister*. Phil Cooper, a sceptical Labour Councillor, did not pull the one punch he threw on the matter: 'We don't trust assurances by officers of the Council'. There was evidently a need for much more careful and open discussion and the ABL report was urgently anticipated. However, fears now grew that – for all we thought we were being engaged and involved to some extent through their offices – the ABL report might be discounted in the Guildhall.

The problem, in essence, was simple. There was within the Guildhall an 'Art Theatre Working Party' (*sic*), under the chairmanship of the Director of Housing and Leisure. This should not be confused with the Arts Working Party of the year before, although for some such a confusion might have been a useful cloak, to avoid any external dagger. It took advice from Alan Giddings of ABL if and when it wanted it, but its business was not made public and it appeared to have no public accountability.

If there were concerns that the theatre issue might degenerate into a party political slanging match, such mystery might have been justified, but this was not the real problem: there were other forces at work. BDP, the developers on behalf of the Prudential, had by now retained the well-known Theatre Projects Limited, run by the redoubtable Iain Mackintosh, as consultants. Theatre Projects, when asked to comment, expressed regret that they were not given the chance to meet with the project architects from BDP before a scheme was drawn up. This scheme, when it was unveiled, placed what was now again being referred to as 'the Arts Centre', in the middle of the commercial development, north of the Hogsmill, with neither river nor street frontage. In their July 1987 report Theatre Projects said, 'Arts Centres provided by developers are generally not successful as arts buildings, the priorities of commercial development and arts provision being somewhat different'. Iain Mackintosh was widely regarded internationally as one of the most astute commentators on how theatre buildings work, and those words have the sound of his voice. Theatre Projects was not retained for the next stage of the development – at who knows what cost in terms of years. Had they been retained, I suspect we would have reached something like our final solution rather more quickly. But these were the days when the borough's officers made decisions and informed everyone else later. Yet another firm of consultants, John Wyckham Associates, was brought in and their initial response was that the Arts Centre was 'being relegated to the backyard of the development'. This assessment apparently did not suit some in the Guildhall and was later watered down, presumably under pressure from somewhere: 'We have been supremely aware of the commercial pressures surrounding the development ... which have resulted in the siting of the proposed arts centre in the position shown', read their final report.

It seems that two processes were going on: one was a public and political engagement which we felt was positive; the other was the progress of a commercial development, encouraged by officers in a process which was not fully accountable. One process would have to give way and by September 1988 the difficulties were coming into the open, with Robin Hutchinson and other opposition members particularly drawing attention to it both on the floor of the Council Chamber and in the press.

In November there was an interesting development: the Prudential took the unusual step of speaking out, in the light of growing criticism. Their spokesperson, Richard Gay, made a detailed statement: 'The working party formed the basis of the brief we were given by the council for designing the scheme. And it is certainly wrong to say that the centre is being relegated to the back yard. It will be the largest single building on the site, and the planning officers were anxious that it should not overwhelm the development'. There was no mention of any in-put from Theatre Projects, nor John Wyckham Associates, and the claim was made that guidance had come, as the statement implies, from council officers. Gay went on to express the hope that work would begin on site in September 1989.

Questions relating to decision-making and accountability were raised again the following year when a potentially divisive move was made, perhaps again unwittingly, by the ruling Conservative group on Kingston Council: the Policy and Resources Committee approved a proposal to sell an area of open space on the River Thames, behind the Ram public house, ostensibly for development. It was known as the Thames Heritage site and was one of the undeveloped open spaces on the river. Tim Harrison was then a local *Surrey Comet* reporter (and, it happens, a well known amateur actor, a formidable pantomime dame). He wrote with a tongue-in-cheek flourish: 'Originally conceived as Kingston's answer to Covent Garden, the square is the last surviving piece of open land between Queen's Promenade in the south and Canbury Gardens in the north'. But it was a spiky issue: 'Money raised from the sale of the land will be used to fund the new 550-seat theatre in the nearby Charter Quay development'. It would not be the last time that the question of funding for the theatre would be blamed on unsatisfactory decisions taken elsewhere.

The ABL report, 'A Review of the Proposed Theatre for the Charter Quay Development in Kingston', was finally published in March 1989. It was fairly comprehensive and was based on six hundred face-to-face interviews and qualitative research with small groups of individuals. An unusually high proportion of Kingston residents attended theatre performances, compared to the rest of Greater London. Many years later, Peter Hall confirmed that on the basis of an audience research survey under his directorship for the National Theatre at about this time, a figure of over 70% of the RNT audience came from what he described as 'the south west toe' of London. Local provision was an attractive proposition: large numbers of people in the ABL survey cited the cost and travelling problems as principal reasons for not going to the West End. ABL's conclusion was that Drama was the preferred type of performance, albeit with a strong music ingredient, with an enterprising, challenging and varied repertoire.

Specific reference was made to the National Theatre as a model: by coincidence, in the light of events a decade and a half later, Sir Peter Hall had just stepped down as Artistic Director of the National, to be succeeded by Richard Eyre. Hall's final year saw his own productions of three of Shakespeare's 'late' plays, *The Tempest*, *The Winter's Tale* and

Cymbeline. It was also the year when the Queen made two dramatic appearances, the first by being the first living monarch to be depicted on stage (in Alan Bennett's *Single Spies*), the second by approving the title 'Royal' on the occasion of the National Theatre's twenty-fifth birthday. Meanwhile, two comments about theatre buildings might have been noted by any authority considering erecting one: Peter Hall's parting shot from the National was that, 'this building in solid concrete will be here for ever and ever, whatever successive governments can do to muck it up. The place exists as a necessary part of the cultural scene of this country'. Another royal – Prince Charles – offered his observation on the newly designated Royal: it was, he said, 'a way of building a nuclear power station in the middle of London without anyone objecting'. Kingston's initial intention, of course, was to demolish its power station and then to build a theatre.

The ABL report recommended that a local repertory company should be established. There should also be provision for a variety of good touring work and access should be given to some local amateur work. A 550 seat theatre, as opposed to 420 seats, would attract a higher quality and greater range of touring work, with also a higher box office potential. The cost to the capital budget was estimated at less than £500,000, and so there were short, medium and long term benefits in the higher capacity. Equally, 550 seats was the maximum capacity given the physical restraints of the site as it was then designated.

The ABL report was received by the Housing and Leisure Services Committee on the 12th July 1989. This included a total capital cost estimate of £6,144,000, which was 'approved'. In addition, £20,000 was assigned as a supplementary revenue sum to allow further work to progress. That £20,000 figure was, in some ways, to play a more significant, practical role in the final analysis than the other larger sums. Interestingly, the annual revenue costs of running the theatre were estimated at £300,000.

The £20,000 was used to set up the Kingston Theatre Trust, viewed initially 'as a fundraising body' to achieve the shortfall between the capital cost and the £4 million allocated by the Council. Its first action was to employ Geoff Howard, then with Arts Business Limited, to advise the Trust. One of Howard's principal tasks was to address the need for strong leadership of the planned fundraising campaign. In November 1989 he visited the renowned broadcaster and Representative Deputy Lieutenant of the Royal Borough of Kingston on Thames, David Jacobs. Jacobs agreed to help assemble and then chair a pilot group to drive the fundraising process. The result was a team of leading (male) figures in the community: Peter Winfield a Kingston resident, racehorse owner and senior partner of Healy & Baker; Tony Anstee the head of the other strand within the Bentall dynasty; Ivan Hannaford pro vice-chancellor for external affairs at Kingston Polytechnic; Peter Jarvis and John Gabb, local businessmen and members of the Mitre Club, an active network for the local business community. The pilot group was also the embryonic membership of the Board of the Kingston Theatre Trust. One woman – Betty, Lady Granchester, head of the Littlewooods Pools family – was approached, for the first of many occasions.

Geoff Howard would shortly, in a quick costume change, transform himself from ABL into a Director of the fundraising consultants Craigmyle. He remained, however, committed to the theatre in dark days and in light and for many years afterwards served as secretary to the KTT. He was paid to work for a day a month, but often gave rather more. His quality was and remained his attention to the detail of company governance and due diligence and he was instrumental in ensuring that the Trust's affairs were conducted appropriately.

In creating Kingston Theatre Trust, the idea was that the Council would be able to keep the management of the theatre project at arms length, supporting it but not controlling it. The Prudential would grant a lease to RBK which would in turn grant a sub-lease to KTT. The Trust would be a company limited by Guarantee, with charitable status. Amongst the lines in the report, accepted by the Council, was the assertion that, 'By providing annual revenue support, the Council would be able to exert considerable practical control. It would also not preclude the Trust from seeking increases if it was thought appropriate'. Such hostages! Such fortunes! But at that particular time the omens seemed positive.

There were to be no fewer than fifteen directors, five of whom would be RBK nominees. In the words of the ABL report 'the board should comprise people with sufficient skill and expertise to be able to run a multi-million pound enterprise, rather than well-intentioned but unknowledgeable people who like the theatre'. If this stark dichotomy held the only two types on offer, I would have to confess to falling into the latter camp.

The Kingston Theatre Trust was incorporated as a company on 1st May 1990, the same month that planning permission was granted for the Prudential scheme. Amongst the subscribers to the Memorandum and Articles of Association were Tony Anstee, of Bentalls; Carl Fisher, a local architect; Ivan Hannaford of Kingston Politechnic; Eileen Gray, a local councillor who had served as Mayor of Kingston. Gray was also a noted cyclist who had campaigned successfully for women's cycling to become a part of the Olympics and was to become one of the fifty members of British Cycling's Hall of Fame and be appointed CBE.

David Jacobs, Peter Winfield, John Gabb and Peter Jarvis were invited to the inaugural Trust meeting along with John McCarthy, the Chairman of the Arts Council, who had served as the Chairman of the Arts Working Party 1986/87. As RBK appointees, Jim Daly, John Clare and Chris Hunt represented the Conservatives, Derek Osborne, the newly named Liberal Democrats and Robin Hutchinson, the Labour Party. Of these political figures, Hutchinson had been campaigning for years to build a theatre; the Tory Jim Daly was keen and mustered the support of his colleagues; the Liberal Democrat Derek Osborne was to play an important role a decade and a half later as Leader of the Council, but in the early days rarely if ever attended a meeting. Geoff Howard was also added to the list of trustees in a temporary capacity.

There were shadows of scepticism from the outset: one of the Guildhall officers attempted to play the puppet-master, trying to persuade Geoff Howard to pull the first meeting which, fortunately, Howard refused to do. That same officer was not infrequently a source of irritation to those trying to move the project forwards.

Meanwhile, as KTT was coming into being, on a site twenty two miles down the Thames, just to the south of Southwark Bridge, where planning permission for a multi-storey office block had been granted, work was suspended while the Museum of London conducted an archaeological dig.

6
A Theatre Trust and a Question of Trust

At the inaugural meeting of the Kingston Theatre Trust on the 29th of November 1990 at the Guildhall, it was suggested that the first aims should be 'to promote, maintain, improve and advance education particularly by the encouragement of the Arts including the arts of drama, mime, opera, ballet, music, singing, dance, literature, sculpture and painting'. I suspect that some current trustees might raise an eyebrow at the breadth of the canvas, but they were not particularly original: almost the same wording had been attached as the objectives of the Overground Trustees in 1978 as a general 'embrace all' for funding applications. But in 1990, for the officers of the Council and any wary councillors lending their support, KTT's aim was principally to raise some £2 million, to bridge the gap in the capital budget.

The official minutes of the meeting suggest that it ran its formal course without particular incident. The first item on the agenda was the election of a Chairman. What the minutes do not record is that Robin Hutchinson interjected before the agenda was addressed, in a manner which was characteristic, at least for those who knew him (and at this meeting only his fellow councillors did, some of whom had been stung by him before). Who were the assembled, he wanted to know? Who had invited them and why? Whom did they represent? Why was no advanced notice of names given? And, in a riff which would have amused himself, but left the meeting baffled: where was Frank Whately? Frank who? Later, Hutchinson was to demand to know the mechanism by which the Directors had been chosen. Over the years his combativeness, sometimes misunderstood as waspishness, was to be of inestimable value, though not everyone was comfortable with it, nor appreciated it. What David Jacobs made of it is not recorded, nor would any misgivings he might have had at that moment have found public record, such was his personal discretion. However, the first Minute of the meeting records that 'Robin Hutchinson proposed that David Jacobs be appointed Chairman' and so began an association between two individuals who were to play such important roles over the coming years.

David Jacobs was by then rather more than the sometime disc jockey – probably the first DJ, it must be said – of 'Juke Box Jury' fame, the BBC's original TV pop music show. He was still broadcasting, as he would until weeks before his death nearly thirty years later, and had become something of a national institution. This had been recognised in his appointment as the Queen's representative in the Royal Borough. He had embraced this duty with the same enthusiasm and selfless devotion which he was to bring to the pursuit of a theatre. Jacobs was to refer to it always as 'our theatre' throughout the many years he presided over a non-existent building. It thus became in its unreality an incontrovertible: it was going to happen, and no matter how long it took, that was that, as far as Jacobs was concerned! It was Kingston's theatre and Kingston would have it!

No reflection on why Kingston finally has its theatre is complete without the recognition of the dogged determination, allied to the charm and a certain ingenuous quality, with which David Jacobs engaged in what he saw as his responsibility as Chairman of the Board of Directors of Kingston Theatre Trust. He was always to be addressed as 'Chairman, if you don't mind'; by nature scrupulously polite, David would only show irritation if he was addressed as 'Chair': 'I'm not a piece of furniture', he would say to an official, who would be thrown temporarily off their stride. If he made some mistakes (and he did sometimes announce appointments or agree to recommendations without the fullest discussion, usually out of a sort of generosity of spirit), even the most sceptical found themselves carried along by his selfless determination.

Having appointed a Chairman, the meeting also records the first resignation, that of Eileen Gray – the renowned cyclist and only woman

– who stepped away 'due to the Royal Borough of Kingston changing its nominees'. Her contribution in a number of ways would have been valuable.

Peter Taunton, one of the Guildhall department chiefs, briefed the meeting: 'the shell of the Theatre would be provided by Prudential and fitted out by the Council, who had committed assistance worth £4.5 million. A further £1.5 million would need to be raised through an appeal which would be the responsibility of the Trust. The Trust would work hand in hand in an advisory capacity with the Council on the fitting out. The Trust would be responsible for the policy of the Theatre and employment of all its personnel'.

It was at this point that Mark Gilks, the Borough's Director of Development, dropped a gentle grenade into the proceedings: the Prudential had put the Charter Quay project on hold; however, he 'was confident that it would go ahead'. So, despite the apparently auspicious messages accompanying its conception it was, in point of fact, very nearly strangled at birth. This was why Peter Taunton, Director of Housing and Leisure, had contacted Geoff Howard in the days immediately preceding the meeting to ask him to cancel or at least postpone it. To his credit, Howard argued that the Trust had been incorporated and the meeting had been called: it should go ahead.

The Prudential's notice was the first set back for KTT, but by no means the last. They had clearly been exercised by some of the criticisms voiced about their scheme, but it was the change in the financial climate which caused the halt: plans might have begun to unravel as the winds of recession blew and meetings between them and the RBK would become less frequent. Crucially, however, KTT demanded to remain in existence and RBK had the foresight both to agree and to retain the services of Howard so that the business of the Trust could continue. As the years went on, the refusal of David Jacobs and some of his trustees to accept what sometimes appeared to be an inevitable demise meant that the flag was kept on the upper half of the mast.

The first meeting drew to a close. Hutchinson, presumably returning to his un-minuted point at the beginning of the meeting, proposed in Any Other Business 'that Frank Whately become a Director'. His proposal was seconded by Jim Daly, a man who retained traces in his accent of his north-eastern background. Jim often thereafter referred to me absent-mindedly as 'Kevin' and I would wonder whether he was disappointed when he first set eyes on me, rather than my brother, at the next KTT Board meeting. As it was, the Chairman began as he would go on and accepted the nomination without question as it came from one of his trustees.

In London, meanwhile, audiences had been stirred by the Royal Court's production of *Our Country's Good*, a play which argues strongly that theatre is a renewing force, and by *Miss Saigon* directed by the young Nick Hytner and which ran for ten years. The new Peter Hall Company began life in New York with Vanessa Redgrave in *Orpheus Descending* and *The Merchant of Venice*, starring Dustin Hoffman, before Hall returned to London and directed a searing production of Ibsen's *The Wild Duck*, with Alex Jennings, Nichola McAuliffe, Alan Dobie, David Threlfall, Lionel Jeffries, Frances Cuka and Terence Rigby in the cast. Neither Hall nor anyone else had an inkling that the movement of the stars would lead him to Kingston more than a decade later.

The Board did not meet again until the following March. This second meeting of the Trust on 7th March 1991 was a gloomy affair, held in the Hotel Antoinette. Nevertheless, at least there was now a politically impartial group in existence to challenge and to suggest, to question and contribute. From my point of view, one of the more memorable aspects of the March KTT meeting was my first encounter with Ivan Hannaford. Our friendship developed through the years when Kingston Polytechnic became a University and we had fruitful conversations up until his sad and untimely death. He had wide-ranging interests, and was then working on his book *Race: the History of an Idea in the West*. He was also a governor of Guildford School of Acting and we went together to student performances there. He was also my first proper personal contact with the institution which would play such an important role in the realisation of the Rose and also, subsequently, in my career.

At the meeting the RBK's Director of Development, Mark Gilks, outlined a current situation which was tempered by the expectation in the construction industry that the economic climate would worsen before it began to get better. This was my first encounter with Gilks. The impression was of a confident, competent and articulate person, but also of a man somewhat detached, a man who enjoyed his status as a Guildhall mandarin, but without flesh and blood conviction. He was to remain in Kingston for a further four years before he moved on to Camden and later became Chief Executive to the London Borough of Hounslow. His words, as reflected in the Minutes of the meeting, seemed unequivocal: 'the siting of the theatre might need to be changed', and the 'viability of the scheme was an important consideration which would be looked at from all angles'. He did, however, affirm that 'the Council's commitment to the theatre remained unchanged'.

Equally evident was that several Directors were concerned that the theatre project might not mature unless pro-active steps were made. One, however, 'felt that the Trust should await further details on the Prudential's revised proposals' and the acting chairman, Jim Daly, 'preferred to defer any decisions on action until the next meeting'. And so the KTT Board and its members began to define themselves.

In point of fact, an action group met again quickly, hosted by Tony Anstee, and issued a press release that 'in the light of the Prudential's decision not to proceed with the Charter Quay development' we were 'resolved to prepare constructive suggestions ... as to how the proposals may be re-planned still to yield a theatre ...'. The release was planned to coincide with the public announcement from the Prudential that they were not proceeding with their multi-million pound Charter Quay development in Kingston upon Thames. The Pru's press release of 16th April 1991 went on to say that, 'Unfortunately, the investment and letting markets have weakened ... These factors together with other unresolved points of detail about the scheme have made it unviable at this time ... We are now considering a more modest redevelopment of the property'. Fortunately, over the years ahead, those who were pro-active were invariably in the ascendant.

What were 'the other unresolved points of detail'? For all the assurances to KTT and subsequent public pronouncements, there seemed to be something we had not been shown. The Prudential had, in fact, written to the RBK in February that, 'whilst the acuteness of the financial viability problem might only be a relatively short term phenomenon I cannot see the other factors readily resolving themselves and I think you must regard our decision as one of abandonment rather than deferral of that scheme'. The missive went further: the Prudential had 'reservations over whether it remains realistic for your Council to continue thinking in terms of commercial development of the area being likely to be capable of sustaining the provision of the Theatre by way of planning gain. In the short-term at least, the prospect of this must be virtually non-existent ... we would urge your Council to re-examine its planning priorities for the area and perhaps consider lowering its horizons as to what it might expect to achieve'.

The details of this letter only became available following a leak to the *Surrey Comet* two months later and Robin Hutchinson's nagging questioning of the Leader of the Council, Paul Clokie, in a Council Meeting in late April. In his reply, Clokie had re-affirmed the Council's commitment that the development should 'provide the Riverside Walk, *a public leisure facility, in preference a theatre* ... provided, *if possible*, as a result of planning gain' (the italics are mine). It was an early sign of political slippage.

There had already been a concern, when the Prudential letter came to light, to discover more about 'the other factors' mentioned as problems unlikely to be resolved. Peter Winfield, acting as an ambassador for the Trust (as he was often to do in the coming years) met with Mark Gilks to see if there was a way that RBK could be more flexible with its planning requirements. At the KTT Board meeting on 1st May 1991 – held, for the first time, at Kingston Polytechnic in the year before it became Kingston University – Winfield reported a 'very encouraging response' and suggested that Gilks, who was in attendance, address the Board. Gilks began by warning us not to be misled by recent articles in the press. I could not help but feel a little patronised. He went on to assert that 'the Council's intention to secure planning gains is *not negotiable*. The Theatre, riverside walk and bridge over the creek are all part of the unitary development plan'. Gilks' 'non-negotiability' was not entirely at one with Clokie's 'if possible', but the question of planning gain was here to stay – an idea which perhaps helped to act as a loophole when the commitment to £4million in the capital budget began to shift. When asked which of the 'gains' would take precedence should the Council be forced to concede on any points, Gilks was adamant that all three would be needed. Perhaps Clokie's 'public leisure facility' was, after all, an honest synonym for 'theatre'. But the Board was showing some clout and was not content to take all at face value. The minutes of the meeting record 'dismay' at the lack of information fed to the Board by the Borough.

Gilks also highlighted that the development might continue in phases. Hopeful as that might sound, there were inevitably worrying concerns: which phase would the theatre be in? It was difficult to think that it might be a priority for either the Council or the Prudential. Years later someone confided in me a conversation which he had had with Mark Gilks, who had said his real ambition for Kingston – a perfectly admirable one – was to complete the opening of the riverside from Kingston Bridge to the Queen's Reach. However, should the theatre plan at any time have threatened to compromise this conjunction, I wonder which path would have prevailed.

The Trust, for its part, continued to flex its muscle. A further working party of Jim Daly, John McCarthy, Geoff Howard and me met on 10th May and agreed to a set of recommendations which we would take to the next full Board meeting. The importance of these recommendations was that we would begin to take control of destiny, rather than merely being the recipients of information on the whim of council officers. We determined short-term and mid-term actions, which would both define the role of the Trust and mean that we would take a measure of control. For any given proposed action, we also determined the means to effect it so that it would be established and not be merely aspirational.

We would agree a brief containing the minimum requirements for a theatre. This was the first step, as far as I was concerned, to settle the confusion of arts centre/ theatre: Kingston would have a theatre. We would begin to outline artistic and management policy. We would agree a public relations strategy, which would not be subservient to others, nor would it function in the slip-stream of events. Finally, we would continue to look at alternative sites, so we would not remain in thrall to the Prudential and their responses to the economic climate or to anything else that hindered them, nor to the interpretation that others might make of those things. In terms of the servicing and resourcing of the Trust, while there was inevitably a resource reliance on RBK, we should be seen to operate as an independent body. Following the meeting, a press release on 6th June 1991 to *The Surrey Comet* affirmed 'Kingston will have a theatre'.

Not satisfied entirely by verbal reports given at Board meetings, Peter Winfield got written confirmation from Mark Gilks about the commitment to the theatre. As ever, Gilks' words were carefully chosen and implied a hierarchy of involvement: 'I was pleased to read of your continuing support for the Council's aspirations relative to the development of the Charter Quay site and the theatre in particular …' This response could only reinforce our determination to take more control and, indeed, make the running.

Our resolve was quickly justified in the light of what next emerged from the political leadership. David Jacobs had written on the 14th May to the Leader of the Council, Paul Clokie, asking him to clarify his reference to 'a public leisure facility, in preference a theatre'. Over a month later, Clokie replied in the most slippery of terms: 'At the present time, it is the intention of the Council to fit out a shell, if it is provided, for a Theatre'. So much for leadership and commitment! Who would be held responsible if 'it' was not provided? What might the Council's 'intention' be next week? The capital commitment to build a theatre had become an 'intention … to fit out a shell, if it is provided'. He then added insult by saying that, 'I feel that the potential of the Assembly Rooms on the corner of Maple Road should be re-examined before any final decisions are made, since it might be possible … to consider a Theatre/Arts complex approach within that building, to which the Trust might become attached'. He concluded his letter: 'May I assure you that contrary to some rumours, the Conservative Group has taken no decision to "kill off" the Theatre'. Heaven forbid that the Trust should give credence to such wild rumour!

At around this time I was asked to play a role in a local charity pantomime, directed by Robin Hutchinson; it was *Snow White and the Seven Dwarfs*, and I was to be a dwarf. On my knees, I led the little fellows onto the stage, carrying cartoon flowers, and sang the verse of the Dwarf's song allocated to me:

I'm Clokie, you've guessed,
I'm in charge of the rest
I've got wit,
I've got charm,
I've got power,
No ifs and no buts,
I like making cuts –
Please allow me to cut you this flower!

The lyrics are rightly forgotten, but I'm glad to reflect that some subsequent Leaders of the Council showed a clearer ambition to bring a theatre to Kingston.

Any notion that the Trust would meet every once in a while and act as a sounding board or piece of blotting paper was put to rest. We gathered again in June and swiftly rebutted the Assembly Room ploy: we had looked at this four years before in the working party and had rejected it; now we were going to create an important theatre in the heart of Kingston, and not try to patch together an unsuitable building – albeit one with an attractive Victorian façade – on the outskirts. David Jacobs asked me to draft a letter which would be sent to Clokie: it was not only a response to his suggestion, but an assertion that the Trust was going to be independent and would not mince words. The directors 'firmly and unanimously' rejected the Assembly Rooms as 'completely unacceptable'. Furthermore, they were 'resolved to have the theatre on the riverside site'. The theatre 'must be central to the heart of Kingston'. The arguments for a theatre in the centre of Kingston 'have been fully deployed several times in the past'. However, we nevertheless repeated them: it would complete the regeneration of the town centre; it would facilitate the commercial and social intercourse between business and the theatre, restaurants and other leisure facilities: 'the one feeds upon the other'. There was a certain self-conscious zeal as this part of the letter moved towards a conclusion: the development of trade, commerce and educational facilities would be complemented by 'the instilling of a soul or spirit to enhance the cultural life of the Royal Borough and provide a real source of enterprise and pride'. There was a rhetorical appeal to a character that was probably not there at the political helm: 'Courage and vision are required in difficult times to make courageous and bold decisions for the long term future'; we should move forward on 'the basis of reason and principle and not temporary expediency'.

The letter then turned to the question of on-going funding of the Trust: we had put in place a strategy for a theatre appeal on which as yet we could not move: it was, in Peter Winfield's words, on 'active hold', a phrase which we would return to many times in the future, if there was a danger of losing momentum. We wanted to review all the proposals made in recent years and develop a clear plan of 'minimum requirements' for the theatre. We were going to force the issue: 'it is anticipated that the Borough will be happy for the fundraising budget to be applied to servicing the broader activities of the Trust' and we asked for 'a marginal increase' in this, which we would discuss with the Leader of the Council at a meeting he had proposed 'after the summer break'.

In fact we pushed ahead with our work on 'Minimum Requirements for a Theatre in Kingston' devised by an action group which included Jim Daly, Tony Anstee, Robin Hutchinson, John McCarthy and me. By the end of August, and thanks in considerable measure to Geoff Howard's loose interpretation of his contracted time, a paper was ready for approval at the September meeting of the Board of Directors of the Trust. It drew on some of the work done by ABL and also of John Wyckham Associates, who had replaced Theatre Projects Limited as Theatre Consultants on the project as it was developed with the Prudential. The ostensible purpose of the 'Minimum Requirements' was to focus the Borough and re-engage the public. They also served to clarify minds within the Trust.

Taking precedence in the list of the Artistic Quality Requirements were: 'good quality professional work which is both attractive and challenging'; the work should be 'primarily drama'; this should include 'drama produced in-house'. It also anticipated work by other companies, 'including drama, opera and dance'. It highlighted the need to offer, 'work which is specially aimed at children in line with the current renaissance of quality professional work'. This was a much clearer definition than had been given by the Working Party, and it certainly moved the emphasis away somewhat from community work. However, by focusing the ambition in this way, I am convinced that it kept the project on track: we were beginning to develop something which was distinctive and would be unique to Kingston. Perhaps not since the seven Saxon kings and King John's Royal Charter would Kingston have such a tangible focus for its civic pride!

There is a detail which suggests the Trust was recognizing the need to be politically astute and to appeal to all shades of opinion, which is appropriate: the theatre must 'enhance the status of Kingston both as a major regional resource for environment and leisure and in terms of its heritage'. The importance of a central location was re-affirmed, although the Trust would 'be flexible as to where the Theatre is provided'. Finally, with regard to design, the idea of the Rose had not yet taken seed: 'In general terms, the Trust requires a theatre of an 'end-on'/ proscenium arch style'.

My own personal thoughts began to be rearranged with regard to design a few months later when I took my NYMT production of *October's Children* to the Swan Theatre, Stratford as a part of the Stratford Winter Season. I enlarge on this impact in Chapter 9.

Meanwhile, our Artistic Quality paper was presented to the Kingston Theatre Trust at the September Board meeting, with officers of the Borough in attendance as usual. To our irritation, the question of an alternative site – by inference the Assembly Rooms – was again raised by Peter Taunton, the Director of Housing and Leisure. He was asked to take the Board's clearly stated views to the Leisure Committee, along with the Action Group's paper. The Assembly Rooms held no interest for us.

Mark Gilks reported that the position with regard to the Prudential had not changed, nor had there been any market movements, but Peter Winfield – alert to the needs to keep everyone 'on-side' – called for a vote of thanks to Gilks 'for the way he had represented the interests of the Theatre'. I was coming to enjoy those moments at every meeting when Winfield, with a twinkle in his eye, would deliver comments, criticisms and encouragements with perception and a disguised but razor-sharp irony. One knew when it was coming: he would begin, 'Mr. Chairman, if I may – ' and then would pause to allow his tongue to push between his lips as he gathered his thoughts, breathing in fully and then delivering.

Sometimes it was to challenge a point; sometimes to offer a loophole in a deadlock; sometimes apparently to offer a compliment which concealed criticism if the object did not adhere to a particular path; sometimes to slice through some bureaucratic equivocation: it was always done in beautifully modulated tones. On this occasion, it was also agreed that Winfield should meet with Gilks before the next meeting – a happy precaution – and that he would also meet with the Prudential.

The meeting with the Leader of the Council had already taken place, owing to the imminent departure into retirement of the Chief Executive, Robert McCloy. Whilst McCloy never had the sort of impact that one of his successors, Bruce Macdonald, was to have he nevertheless enjoyed projects which might bring prestige to the Borough, with attaching reflected personal glory. The meeting was indeterminate of outcome, but of more concern was what impact McCloy's successor would have.

The Action Group met to develop a public relations strategy. Its importance resides in the fact that from that point onwards there was pro-active and focused engagement with getting the theatre story into the press, initially locally, but soon into the regional and national media too. The idea was to keep the pressure on, so that there would be no wavering. It began to work: in a feature headed 'Theatre hopes still alive', the *Surrey Comet* responded to an early press release saying 'Despite the setbacks, campaigners are continuing their efforts to ensure that Kingston will one day have its own theatre'. It went on to say that the developers have 'not ruled out the possibility that it may still go ahead'. The article gave an outline of our minimum requirements, giving substance to the aspiration.

There were other little steps forward: the Housing and Leisure Committee accepted our minimum requirements which was both important in its own right, but also indicative of a mood, if not in the Leader's room, at least in the Council, that the Trust would be listened to and our thoughts adopted. As far as possible in a situation so responsive to a difficult downturn, we seemed to be making the pace.

Robin Hutchinson's work in the Council was crucial in this respect. My only concern was that he would finally become bored with the tedium of work as a councillor and so the theatre project might lose its cutting teeth in Council: he had the intellect and stamina and relentless energy to play a long game, but could sometimes and without warning simply become interested in something else. It is difficult to estimate fully what he achieved: he did get bored, but fortunately it was only with the Council. Off the Council, he found himself freer to use his developing ingenuity, particularly in collaring the right people at the right time.

Meanwhile, 'the project is seen as live and under regular review' was the message from both Gilks and Peter Winfield, reporting at the November Trust meeting on the current state of the Prudential's thinking. In the coming years it was to be a question of how this same sentiment could be expressed in different ways whilst keeping some sense of progress. But the Prudential was now aware that the theatre would not go away. In the light of markets, the Pru was beginning to think in terms of a site with offices and some shops, rather than shops and some offices. Most on the Trust had no particular opinion until Winfield observed that letting on the site might be more successfully achieved with retail lots, although offices had the potential to bring in higher revenue. Perhaps it should concern the Trust if it led to any political falling out.

There was another caveat which we chose not to discuss in detail, on the grounds that the time was not right. John McCarthy, who gave the impression of being a sort of twentieth century John Aubrey type who liked to poke around in this and that, had made a particular visit to Richmond Theatre to discuss with them their fundraising for the £4 million renovation which was underway in the beautiful – but not particularly comfortable – Frank Matcham designed theatre, which first opened in 1899. In this Grade II listed building it was principally lavish restoration of Matcham's work which had cost the money, although there were some additions to the building as it stood. McCarthy made two points: should their appeal spill over our boundaries at a time when we need to go to the public, ours might suffer; also, rich Richmond was having difficulties raising money from their public. It was a gentle rumble of thunder moving towards Kingston.

In early January 1992 a number of us represented the Trust in a meeting with the Borough's new Chief Executive, Timothy Hornsby. David Jacobs felt that the meeting had achieved its objective – that the Trust was here to stay and 'meant business'. Hornsby was a striking character, engaging and erudite. Some years later, he was described in *The Guardian* as 'a tall, dandyish figure hurrying along [like] an actor on his way to a performance ... Timothy Hornsby is witty enough to ad lib in a Sheridan classic'. It would have been interesting to see what role he might have played in the theatre saga had he stayed in Kingston. As it was, he soon moved on and reappeared as the Chief Executive of the National Lottery Board. It was an irony: we were to spend a number of years jumping through the hoops of John Major's Lottery creation. For many on Kingston Council, the Lottery would quickly become the preferred alternative source of funding to the £4 million promised by RBK in 1988. In the upshot, nothing of any significance flowed Kingston's way from this source.

The Lottery cropped up for the first time at our May 1992 meeting. Kenneth Baker, then Home Secretary, had in March introduced the Lottery Bill in the Commons. Amongst many other things, it would consider support for 'worthwhile new buildings'. Peter Taunton reminded the Board – and, I now reflect, perhaps ominously – that when the authority had first made its capital commitment it had anticipated also a revenue support requirement of £250,000 - £400,000: this would need to be reviewed as the artistic policy of the theatre developed. Perhaps there were already thoughts of depositing obligations elsewhere.

In addition to the Lottery, which would become our own red herring, there was still no sign of movement from the Prudential. They had always had the option of selling their majority part of the site on to another developer, although they appeared still to favour doing the development themselves albeit without being able to anticipate when that might be. It was disappointing, too, that in the Council's Unitary Development Plan for the site published in March 1992 there was no reference to 'theatre' but a reversion to 'Arts Centre' and even that in parenthesis. Gilks agreed 'to do whatever he could' – as though he was not the chief officer and responsible – to ensure that reference to 'the theatre' was always visible in documentation.

David Jacobs wrote to David Mellor, the Secretary of State for National Heritage, following the call for responses at the publication of the Lottery White Paper. We had registered Kingston's theatre at national level as a potential recipient, although it was not expected that any money would come on stream until 1994.

As the summer wore on, there was an interesting diversion: Peter Winfield had received a proposal from a local property consultant by the name of Peter Woods suggesting 'a modest new Arts Centre' on one of the riverside sites not under Prudential control. This was not the first time a proposal like this had been made. The previous year a proposal from Omenport to build some sort of arts facility near the station had been dismissed as not serious. This new proposal, offering a space of some 250-300 seats, was for a very much less ambitious theatre than that which we were now determined upon. The approach had been made to the Trust rather than the Council which allowed us to preen our feathers. Dismissing it gave us the opportunity of restating our determination that our new theatre would be 'an important regional centre' whilst making a fundamental contribution to the regeneration of evening and weekend life in the town centre.

From November 1992, whilst Board meetings continued to be held in the same room, it was now at Kingston University, rather than Kingston Polytechnic. There is no doubt that the change of status would bring a range of benefits which would prove to be of inestimable value to the theatre project. Indeed, it can be argued that the theatre might not have been realised without the University, and certainly not in the way that it did.

As 1993 dawned so also did a little light begin to shine on our stage: the economic climate seemed to be easing a little. The Prudential was working up a scheme which included a new mix of elements, but with housing a central feature and Woolworths had entered discussions. Peter Winfield, with characteristic understatement, decided that the economic viability of the new scheme, along with prospects for the theatre, was 'not unhopeful'. Importantly, too, our minimum requirements remained in tact. It was all still at feasibility level, but there was just the feeling we might be on the move. Meanwhile, the Council's Leisure Committee had received our report favourably. Added to all of this, an advertisement appeared in *The Guardian*, on Monday 15th March 1993:

Arts Development Officer: (One Year fixed term contract) We are offering an exciting opportunity for an arts professional to work in Kingston's Leisure Services Department ...

On the face of it, small beer and a temporary appointment; however, it would lead a year later, to the placement of anything but in the person of Colin Bloxham, another to join the band of those who had ambition and who would not let go.

7
Flowering Confidence

The Kingston Theatre Trust sat tight through the years of recession in the early nineties. At national level, the Sterling Crisis leading to 'Black Wednesday', 16th September 1992, was focusing the mind of Kingston's M.P., the Chancellor of the Exchequer Norman Lamont, which is perhaps why he expressed so little interest in the attempts to improve the cultural climate of his constituency.

In the late nineteen eighties, I had been researching an idea for a piece of musical theatre for young people, a project which took me, David Nield and Jeremy James Taylor to the Soviet Union, on behalf of the National Youth Music Theatre. Mikhail Gorbachev was the country's leader as General Secretary of the Communist Party and had introduced the concept of *perestroika*, which was supposed to be overcoming stagnation in the Soviet economy. We wrote *October's Children* (mentioned in Chapter 6) which, following performances at the Edinburgh International Festival, was then invited by the RSC to play at the Swan Theatre, Stratford for a week in February 1991 as a part of their Visitors' Season. Working in the Swan was a revelation. This beautiful space, with an audience capacity of around 450, allowed for both intimate scenes and epic demonstration: it is an exhilarating place for audiences and spectators.

The Swan had had its own serendipitous evolution up until its opening in 1986. The RSC had used what was known as the Conference Room as a rehearsal space more or less since its foundation in 1961. Actors and directors had always found it a comfortable space in which to work and moving productions from this rehearsal base to the sprawling expanse of the Memorial Theatre had often been a trying experience. Trevor Nunn wanted a theatre to fill the gulf between the Memorial Theatre and the tiny Other Place. At some point he realised that the Conference Room was, in point of fact, the building gutted by fire in 1926: it was the original Stratford Shakespeare Theatre. Nunn, along with the designer John Napier and the architect Michael Reardon, developed a theatre loosely based on an idea of an Elizabethan theatre with a thrust stage. Their attempts to raise money came to nothing and the project was shelved until, several years later a chance encounter with a philanthropist from the United States, Fred Koch, led to all the money for the project coming into place in one fell swoop. The Swan Theatre in Stratford is a jewel: its special quality is the relationship between the actors and the audience: Reardon wanted to create an acting platform, as he said in a chapter of *This Golden Round* (1989), 'modelled on the forestage of an Elizabethan theatre' and to 'recreate the relationship between actor and spectator when both are contained within a common architectural framework'. Whilst the discovery of the archaeology of the original Rose only a year or two after the Swan was built showed Reardon was not entirely accurate in his assumption about the nature of the Elizabethan forestage, the Swan, nevertheless, offers a wonderful actor/audience experience, which my young company relished.

Meanwhile, the national financial crisis did not stop Sam Wanamaker's Globe project making headway. Soon, there was activity on the Globe's Southbank site, close to where the archaeology of the Rose had been discovered in 1989. By the Spring and Summer of 1993, a number of Globe events were taking place on a makeshift stage and work began on erecting some of the wooden bays which would eventually realise Wanamaker's dream of rebuilding Shakespeare's theatre. It captured the imagination of my students and me and we became members of 'Globelink', a means for young people to become involved in the developing project. We contributed performances to profile-raising days, and buried on site time-capsules with various artefacts relating to our productions. A recording of the Tiffin School production of *The Comedy of Errors* was played from time to time in the Globe Centre while the building continued. But alas, by the end of December 1993 Sam had died, cruelly taken away before he could see the finished result of his lifetime's passion.

Sam's legacy is the beautiful Globe, which is one of the most successful commercial theatres in the country. But it was also to make its contribution to what we began constructing in Kingston three years after the Queen opened the finished Globe in 1997. Wanamaker had refused to bow to what others might have called the inevitable and in doing so was creating a new theatre which had its reference point firmly in a past which had been a golden age of English drama.

Meanwhile, theatre across the country was facing a mounting crisis. The Arts Council's annual report for 1993/4 gave out an emergency call: 'One of the nation's greatest assets, its provincial theatres, remains on the brink of an irreversible spiral of decline ... repertory theatres must evolve or die'. It was ten years since the publication of the Arts Council's *The Glory of the Garden*, the first major review made of its work since its founding shortly after the Second World War. In this, the discrepancy between London and the regions had been exposed, yet in the intervening decade little seemed to have changed. Peter Hall used to say that theatre is always in decline and always has been, which you can take as the words of a pessimist or a realist. After all, the original 1587 Rose theatre on the Southbank flourished in the 1590s, but was closed by 1603/4. The Globe did not survive the closure of the theatres in 1642. Most of the great Victorian music halls have gone – and so on. However, in the early 1990s regional theatres were struggling to survive and having to diversify into programmes and community activities which made them a very different animal to the repertory playhouse. This, in itself, was not necessarily a bad thing, but it did signal difficult times for in-house repertory theatre and was not a fertile situation for anyone harbouring a desire to create a new theatre with aspirations to create new work.

Other theatre work flourished and not only in London. The emergent companies of ten years before were now producing a range of radical and exciting work and vying for attention. Complicité, led principally by Simon McBurney, began to make work of astonishing originality: *The Street of Crocodiles* and *The Three Lives of Lucy Cabrol* captured the imagination and marked a significant development of what was known, after Artaud, as 'total theatre'. When *Out of a House Walked a Man* was played on the National's Lyttleton stage in 1994, it was recognised that Complicité was of international significance. Kneehigh Theatre, which had started weaving its tales in the early 1980s making work for children, soon found that they were breaking boundaries, with challenging and sensitive work which explored the human condition with a dramatic integrity and innocence which embraced audiences of all sorts. While they never lost their Cornish roots, they gained a national prominence which must have caused ambivalent feelings in their self-effacing founder and joint artistic director, Mike Shepherd. Nor had Kneehigh ever lost its appeal to young people. These were amongst the best of a range of companies rightly making demands on funding in a difficult economic climate, characterised by fewer and smaller grants and the consequent reduction in the availability of quality touring work.

In June 1994 the Kingston Theatre Trust published its latest mission statement. The theatre should be capable of offering, 'good quality professional work which is both attractive and challenging' and it should offer 'primarily drama', some of which must be 'produced in-house'. The question of how much access would be given to community groups to *perform* in the theatre remained ambiguous: the artistic policy should seek to develop 'a close and fruitful relationship with the community in order to monitor community needs and the change in tastes'.

It was not a good time to be trying to build a new theatre building. However, plans were revived. Early in 1994, the Prudential began to produce a new series of feasibility drawings for Charter Quay which now favoured residential development, a dramatic change from the last scheme which had been primarily commercial. One of the two minor landowners of the site, Friends Provident, indicated they were not willing to contribute to the site development. Peter Winfield tried unsuccessfully to act as a broker, but there was a general resignation to the likelihood of placing a compulsory purchase order on Friends Provident land.

Winfield was, in his inimitable way, scathing of the Friends Provident response when the Board met in early March 1994. It was, he said, cynically commercial: they did not have to invest in development proposals as they would get their profit anyway. However, there was general delight that at last we seemed to be on the move again, although we were wary of another false dawn. Nevertheless, by late in the year, following a presentation of new plans in the Guildhall, Winfield was able to say with a twinkle in his voice, 'the sun will not be behind the clouds forever, and I sensed it peeped out somewhat last night!'

An interesting footnote to the March 1994 KTT Board meeting was a report from Robin Hutchinson that plans for a small arts centre in the south of the borough, the Douglas Centre, were progressing well, and he looked forward to an inaugural reception there which would take place following the May local elections. To this day, the Cornerhouse, as it is now known, thrives as a community arts space.

On the local political front, there had been a change a year earlier in that the Liberal Democrats were now in charge at the Guildhall, and with a workable majority. It seemed then that there would be a fresh political dynamism. The Leader of the Council, John Tilley, was clear in his group's continued support for the theatre: when questioned about the theatre's viability in a difficult financial time when other theatres were under pressure he wrote, 'I would say that a new theatre building in Kingston could reasonably be expected to have a life of over a hundred years and we do, therefore, need to take a long term view and not be too influenced by the fluctuations in the fortunes of theatres in the area'. In a local radio interview soon after the elections in May 1994 he had said that there was a budget for a theatre and that one of his priorities was to ensure that this was placed clearly on the agenda of his administration. We took his words at face value, perhaps naïvely.

There was a contingent hope that the ruling elected councillors would have better control over the permanent officers, and whether by design or good fortune there seemed some promise. One early sign was the appointment of Colin Bloxham as the full time Arts Officer to Kingston. He arrived in early 1995 and quickly demonstrated his breadth and commitment: one of his first tasks was to write the outline brief for ABL's report update, and these reveal his grasp over the essentials. Later, as his portfolio inevitably developed, to an important degree as a result of his tireless activity, he became Principal Arts Officer. Sadly, however, Bloxham was the exception rather than the rule amongst council officers for the time being.

The Prudential had appointed St. George plc in Autumn 1994 as the developer. St. George was a young and quite brash company and had never previously developed a scheme which included a theatre, other than to purchase a 1930s theatre and bingo hall in Brixton and redevelop it as residential flats! They were rapidly making their mark resuscitating urban areas with large residential complexes, notably in Clerkenwell in the City of London. This area of London might have been well known in the Middle Ages for its mystery plays performed by the parish clerks and for the steamy haunts of Shakespeare's Justice Shallow in his youth, but such dramatic pedigree had left no impact on this modern London developer. St George would eventually build the shell of what became the Rose Theatre, but for the time being their architects for the whole project was the firm of Renton, Howard, Wood and Levin (RHWL), and they certainly had a track record in theatre design.

This was a surprise as RBK, the Prudential and KTT expected St. George would return to BDP for the development as a whole, as they knew the site so well. RHWL came fresh from their triumph of winning the competition to build Manchester's new Concert Hall, later to become the Bridgewater Hall. Their work included Woking's New Victoria, the Derngate in Northampton, the Anvil in Basingstoke, the Warwick Arts Centre and – perhaps most interestingly – Sheffield's Crucible. The Crucible, based on Tyrone Guthrie's thrust theatre idea, had opened twenty years earlier. In early 1995 work in Kingston began in earnest again.

In this renewed plan, the Prudential would give the land and St. George would build the shell of the theatre for Kingston. This was not disinterested philanthropy; both would gain materially. St. George would negotiate a Section 106 Planning Agreement with RBK, whereby they would enter into a contract to build the shell of the theatre in exchange for planning permission for the whole site. The proposed schedule of accommodation in fact saw a reduction in the space allocation to the theatre, from the 1990 scheme of 3977 square metres to 3262 square metres in this. However, there would be no movement as far as the seating capacity was concerned: in this scheme it remained at 550 seats.

Robin Derham, then a partner with RHWL, was the architect particularly responsible for the theatre. I think he found some frustrations with
a situation which was anything but clear: whilst KTT should in practice
have been in the client role as far as the theatre was concerned, there
was yet again meddling by the mandarins. Indeed, when in the previous
September I had stressed the importance of the Trust being involved in
advising on theatre matters, the then Director of Housing and Leisure,
Peter Taunton, said the Council would be open to any advice but the
final decision would rest with them. We were not consulted effectively
during the first months of this new development and this led to particular
problems, which could have been avoided before they arose. It was not
clear who in the local authority was taking initiatives without consulting
effectively. Taunton was to have the responsibility for Leisure – and thus,
I suppose, his engagement with the theatre – but I can recall no input
either enlightened or knowledgeable. He was removed from his portfolio
some months later as a result of a local authority internal reorganisation in
which Leisure was transferred to Education, but by then some damage had
been done.

At the same time, there were tensions from the developers, who
evidently liked to get on with things. This did not initially sit comfortably
with KTT: whilst we had an artistic policy, it was only in outline owing
to the uncertainty of the project. In retrospect, we might have been more
proactive in this regard at an earlier stage, although there was a danger
that this would have opened old sores over the arts centre/ theatre
argument and delayed things further. As it was, we needed time to develop
an artistic policy in greater detail and have time with the architect. But
there remained the confusion over who the client was, and at this stage
the Trust was seen as subsidiary. Derham's response was, I suppose,
pragmatic: working to the general 1989 brief, he produced a design for a
relatively simple end-on theatre, with a proscenium, stalls and two circles
in a rough rectangular space, with wings and a fly tower. There was no
evident trace of a Crucible influence. I was surprised that the first working
meeting between Derham and KTT members did not take place until
March 1995, after he had produced his first plans, through no fault of
his: he had, of course, already met with officers from RBK frequently.

Subsequently, he made every effort to accommodate our concerns, and I formed a high regard for his expertise, but his position was never less than difficult.

A KTT Building sub-committee was created, in part because Robin Derham had asked specifically, through RBK, for more input from us. The committee comprised Carl Fisher, himself an architect, as chairman, Tony Anstee, Geoff Howard and me. In early March 1995 we met with the architects, led by Derham, and the developers, led by the St. George MD Tony Carey. Colin Beckenham, the project development administrator, and Colin Bloxham were there on behalf of RBK. The proposal was now to build the theatre immediately to the south of the Hogsmill Creek, with either a back wall onto the High Street, or the side wall of the auditorium. The building would lie parallel to the High Street on an area approximately where the front of the building now stands and along the line of what is currently the service road into Charter Quay. It was evident to us at this meeting that thinking was already fairly advanced, which I found irritating, not least because the thinking about the theatre itself was pedestrian.

I circulated to all members of the KTT some extracts from Iain Mackintosh's very recently published book, *Architecture, Actor & Audience*. Mackintosh was, of course, a senior director with Theatre Projects, a company that had been replaced as consultants in Kingston by council officers several years previously. The American theatre director Gregory Mosher, in a publisher's puff, wrote, 'This is the best book on how architectural design affects our work since Peter Brook's *The Empty Space*'. Mackintosh highlighted two particular dangers: buildings created by directors who, by the time the building was opened, would no longer be there; and buildings made in committee, which could attempt to satisfy all, and end up satisfying no-one. Peter Hall figured in two of his examples: Hall had presided, as Artistic Director of the RSC, over evolving plans for a permanent London base during the late nineteen sixties with his head of design John Bury; Hall had long since departed for the National by the time the Barbican opened in 1982. Hall with Bury then inherited the Olivier Theatre at the National with its characteristics born of its great namesake's particular and problematic point of view. As Mackintosh said: 'Decisions taken years ago by others ... are now, literally, cast in concrete'.

At least Hall would be enthusiastic about Kingston's Rose, when it finally appeared as a shell, although it was not his idea: he and Alison Chitty would oversee the fit-out, but that was nearly a decade later. In the meantime, Mackintosh's critique of the Olivier theatre was instructive: Olivier had decreed that it should be an open stage, with no proscenium, of itself an excellent idea. Olivier had been a player when Tyrone Guthrie began the revival of the Elizabethan stage idea, at Elsinore in 1936. But it was Olivier's second decree that created the problem: no spectator should be able to look across the acting space and see any other spectator. This abandoned a fundamental principle of audiences being 'reminded of themselves'. The result is a vast auditorium, with a width which renders the task of establishing focus on the stage almost impossible. In a statement I thought salutary and disturbing for us, Mackintosh said, 'The committee and the passage of time – in the case of the Barbican as long as seventeen years from conception to opening night – decreed discontinuity'.

An early problem in Kingston was in relation to the siting and orientation of the theatre: Derham insisted on the need to build over the Hogs Mill; indeed, his plan was for the main entrance of the theatre to be on a bridgeway over the little Thames tributary, at the western end of the current Griffin Passage. There would be views from the foyer to the Clattern Bridge and through the Griffin passage to the Market Place. Looking down the Hogsmill, the Thames itself would be glimpsed. If Planning would not grant this, he argued, the foyer area at stalls level would be seriously restricted and it was likely that the rehearsal/ studio space could not be accommodated at all. His foyer design and its aspect were attractive. However, it indirectly gave rise to a second and, from the theatre's point of view, a more significant problem: the visual impact on the High Street was of a blank wall, possibly with the stage door in it.

The pace was beginning to increase, but more quickly than was wise. It is an irony that having waited for so many years, we were now trying to keep the process in check, but there were too many cooks. Rather than being to the fore in developing the project, the Trust found it necessary to engage in the checking and balancing to avoid irredeemable errors. We met again with the architects and developers at the beginning of April to agree a timetable. Once the planning application was submitted, it was anticipated there would be six months of public consultation. Friends Provident was, it seemed, finally about to join in, but not before being faced with a compulsory purchase order. Robin Derham was concerned that our determination to revisit the artistic policy, which also meant considering the updating of the ABL report, might slow the momentum. It *would* do, there was no doubt, but I thought it was important. We were constantly being given the impression that we should accept what was on offer lest it evaporate. In the upshot, of course, this particular building would not finally be realised. However, it had one particular feature we would later make use of as a sort of rising spirit: it contained a fly tower, for which planning permission would eventually be given before the plan collapsed: it was a ghost whose brief glimpse and passing would prove useful in the years to come.

Support for a slower and more considered approach came from an unlikely quarter. The responsibility for Leisure in the borough moved to the Department of Education. The director, Bill Dickinson, wrote to David Jacobs that although discussions were reaching an advanced stage he was concerned about rushed decisions: 'It is my view that your work will be more likely to bear fruit if we do our homework carefully at this stage'. His tone was open and frank: 'I fully appreciate that this letter may seem to be attempting to slow down the current momentum. I wish to assure you, however, that the important work that you and the members of the Kingston Theatre Trust are carrying out on behalf of the Council and the community at large will have my fullest support'. He asked to be kept fully informed, he was willing to meet and so on. At last we had a department director who was getting things into an appropriate perspective. As his designated officer was Colin Bloxham, a mutual trust might reasonably be expected to develop. I trace the particularly fruitful relationship between the parties involved – the Trust and RBK – in the development of the theatre back to this point.

A preliminary draft of costings estimated that the construction of the building alone would come to £5,860,000. With fit-out and professional fees the figure rose to £7 million, excluding tax and two other diverse but interesting factors: production lighting and archaeology. The conscious omission of the former – lighting – is a mystery, but remedied in later years when Richard House joined the Trust. In the light of the experience at Rose Court on the Southbank, the omission of archaeology in Kingston is a little bit of ironic serendipity. Of course, Kingston has been a rich ground for archaeology, not least in areas near the river, so some allowance would have been wise. Our finally completed Rose owes more to archaeological activity further down the Thames than to anything else. The omissions did not remain: the Lottery application in the event took all these factors into account.

On the 15th May 1995, the architects and developers came to their first full board meeting, where the plans were greeted with guarded enthusiasm. Carl Fisher, who chaired the Building Committee at this stage, gave support to the broad outline of the plan. However, while both Derham and Deborah Aplin, the St. George Development Director, talked up the merits of the entrance of the theatre being on the Hogsmill, there was a strong concern in the Trust: as in the 1989 scheme, the theatre might be 'lost' within the larger development.

Thereafter the Building Committee, which expanded to include Robin Hutchinson, Lorraine Monk and David Nield, met regularly. The question of the orientation of the theatre and its High Street presence was continuing to vex minds. I was also concerned about the configuration of the auditorium, but to have attempted major internal changes at this point could have been fatal; fate held its own solution in store. The location was attractive and sympathetic to the aim of creating a cultural heart in the town centre. We were aware that we could not dictate the precise orientation of the building, but there was clearly a divergence between most of us and the architect on the question of the main entrance being on the High Street, where currently Derham had sited the stage door. Our mission statement had been a part of the brief: 'Wherever the Theatre is sited within the Charter Quay area, it is critical that it be accessible and in such a position that it can establish a strong presence within both the day and night life of the Town ...' If Derham found this heel-digging a frustration, he had some justification: the statement concluded, '... and preferably with a visual relationship to the river'. The swans on the

Thames might have periscopic necks, but they don't have to worry about irreconcilables. In fact, by placing the main entrance on the Hogsmill, he had taken some advantage of river views to the Thames. However, a High Street presence became our mantra, which would finally be realised. If only there had been proper consultation early enough to establish priorities this *impasse* would not have been reached – an object lesson in not sheltering a project from proper advice and scrutiny.

In our report to the full Board for its November '95 meeting the profile problem was highlighted, and we suggested acceptance of the designs must be conditional on satisfying that aspect of our mission statement. In addition, I remained uneasy about the rigidity of the proscenium and we added a key condition to the brief that the proscenium should be removable, to allow for adaptation within the space: it was a compromise of sorts, although compromise could in the longer term prove a shackle. We were also having discussions with a variety of potential artistic partners and asked for more substantial additional office space to accommodate them. This was always going to be difficult: the space available was limited to a footprint which we could not expand.

Arts Business Limited had been re-commissioned early in the year to bring their 1989 report up to date. In March '95 KTT had submitted an Advance Notice form to the Arts Council indicating its intention of applying for £5.5m from the National Lottery towards the total capital costs. ABL gave an interim report in early May. There had been some striking changes since 1989, both locally and nationally. Kingston had developed as a retail centre: its sense of subservience to Richmond was a thing of the past, with the opening of John Lewis and the Bentalls Centre. The Market Place was being added to Clarence Street as a car-free zone. The political changes in the Council brought an end finally to one party assuming power on a more-or-less permanent basis, with the accompanying complacence that that situation had nurtured. Most notable, although not highlighted as such by ABL, was the 'growth of the University, and further growth potential'. For the full report they were focusing on artistic policy, revenue costs and the National Lottery application. The legacy of poor priorities persisted: their full report, in June, would go in the first instance not to KTT, but to the Education and Leisure Services Committee in the Guildhall. Almost a month elapsed before we, as KTT members, saw it officially. At a subsequent Board meeting, the deputy Director of Education apologised, blaming 'an administrative error'! In fact, a letter from the Head of Leisure Development, dated 27th June 1995, makes it clear that this was deliberate policy.

Alan Giddings of ABL presented the report to the Trust in late July. Its three principal thrusts related to the artistic policy, the capital programme and the nature and style of management. The theatre could not, he argued, be a full producing house. A recent Green Paper from the Arts Council had concentrated on the need for growth of middle scale touring theatre and that is the area which should complement any other artistic endeavour. In terms of the Lottery bid, we would have to ensure that we sat within the regional and national policy, and not merely compete with other local theatres; enhancing Kingston would not in itself be enough. The thoughts about management were clearly influenced by a growing nervousness about revenue funding in the borough: it should develop a programme that would maximise income potential. However, it did include the need for £3-400,000 of revenue funding a year. It was in other respects neither an exciting nor a particularly enlightening report.

My main concern was that the Lottery had been given such a platform; it was as though we should be driven by what the new kid on the block might approve. I urged that the Trust remember that all parties in the Borough supported the theatre, irrespective of the Lottery. Robin Hutchinson thought that our Artistic sub-committee must get on with its business and take control of where we were going. David Nield argued, in relation to the Lottery, for the development of distinction and originality in our plans. The response of the Director of Planning, Mark Gilks, to our remarks as ever seemed to carry a sub-text: he believed 'that capital money from the Lottery will not only provide urgently needed funds but will also demonstrate the validity of the theatre proposals'. David Jacobs responded sharply: 'If the theatre is not funded by the Lottery, the theatre will still go ahead'. It was at moments like this that Jacobs demonstrated an effective edge, which surprised those only familiar with his public persona as a broadcaster. Genial and affable though he was, and scrupulously polite, he could be uncompromising if he felt this project to which he had become so firmly attached might be threatened.

There was some stimulation from another quarter: further moves were made to bring the University into partnership. The University's trustee was now Keith Grant. Ivan Hannaford remained a trustee, though only for a few months until his sad and quite sudden death. Hannaford had been a constant and wise voice for many years and had established the groundwork which led to Kingston University becoming a major party in the development and success of what became the Rose Theatre.

Grant was a former Director of the Design Council and had recently become Dean of the Faculty of Art and Design. He spoke with the Vice Chancellor Bob Smith who, apparently, expressed interest while making clear that it was unlikely that any funding would be available. There was mention that the teacher training programmes in music and drama might be involved with the building. The scale of ambition was not quite as it was to become under Smith's successor and his retirement was on the near horizon. Grant himself, however, saw more potential. He was clear that for the theatre to achieve its full potential, amateur work should be severely limited and that we should stand firm on our requirements in the development, particularly in having an adaptable auditorium with a removable proscenium.

We began to re-draft the artistic policy and for the first time put an emphasis on the potential for work of national and international significance. It was now that plans began to be fleshed out properly, with artistic aspirations moving to the fore. In the first instance, Robin Hutchinson chaired meetings, and later I took over. In our different ways, we were both driven with the same objective and our collaboration was as fruitful as ever. We had also developed a confidence in ourselves and each other, born of the experience which had developed over the past fifteen years. We recognised that a paramount concern should be to have an artistic identity which both separated us from other theatres in the region, whilst also exciting people. We both wanted to see new work created in Kingston, but recognised that political and financial restrictions were, for the time being, a barrier. Along with David Nield and Geoff Howard, Colin Bloxham was a permanent contributor and, whilst never compromising his position within RBK, was imaginative and constructive: he had begun to epitomise a new approach within the Guildhall. We developed an idea of the theatre becoming a home or second home for a group of medium scale companies capable of creating exciting new work. Certainly Complicité and Kneehigh were in our minds, although no firm moves were made, other than a brief conversation I had with Mike Shepherd of Kneehigh, who was interested.

A focus on work for young people would be spearheaded with the National Youth Music Theatre, for whom David Nield was Chairman and I was an associate writer and director. It was at a time when the work of the NYMT was pre-eminent with an international reputation riding high. Since its establishment under the artistic direction of Jeremy James Taylor in 1985, the work of the NYMT had grown in reputation year by year. *The Ragged Child*, which I wrote with Nield and Taylor, had brought the company international notice: after the Bergen and Edinburgh International Festival performances, the following year we played for six weeks at Sadler's Wells, and shortly afterwards filmed the production for the BBC. That cast had some interesting faces, including Charles Edwards, a young Jude Law who joined his friend Jonny Lee Miller as well as Jo Davies. Later, the same team of Nield, Taylor and Whately created *October's Children* which also went to the International Festival before performances at Sadler's Wells and the Swan, Stratford. In 1993 I began work on an idea for a piece on the Arthurian legends, initially called *The Song of the Loathly Lady* with Peter Allwood and Joanna Billington (née Horton). With Jeremy Taylor joining us, we developed it for the NYMT as *Pendragon* and at the Edinburgh Festival Fringe in 1994 the production won a *Scotsman Fringe First* award before travelling the world. In the summer of 1995 *Pendragon*, along with the NYMT production of *The Threepenny Opera*, arrived on Broadway in the vast City Center theatre where it played to packed houses and was the New York Times' *Critic's Choice*, where it was described as 'a remarkable accomplishment ... In *Pendragon* one visits Britain's mythic past while watching the future of its theater take place'. Young players like Sheridan Smith, Rebecca Lock, Tom Chambers and Madeleine Worrall gained international notice and Andrew Lloyd Webber described the NYMT as 'the best youth music theatre in the world'. At the time, a Kingston collaboration seemed to augur well.

All of this would, of course, necessitate increased administrative space at the least and Geoff Howard suggested that if this meant an increase in the cost of the theatre in order to deliver the policy, then we should signal this early. We recognised that there must be roots in the local community and that there would be some non-professional access, but this would be carefully managed within the balance of the work as a whole and would have to take realistic account of costs. With a particular interest in youth work, we were beginning to develop plans for a summer youth festival. Finally, and this reflected my concern about the internal design and fit-up, it was considered vital that the theatre be designed with flexibility. If all of this gave rise to the sound of slamming stable doors, it was symptomatic of a process which, thankfully, would soon be changed – but not until after the Lottery hoops had been negotiated with varying degrees of success.

8 Handicaps and Hurdles

We began to prepare the Lottery application in 1995. In the theatre further afield, it was the year of *Blasted* and the emergence – sadly so briefly – of Sarah Kane. How fickle a world theatre can be! This play was savaged by most national critics, more virulently than ever even *Waiting for Godot* was forty years before. Kane now, not unlike Beckett, is eulogised and most of those critics have recanted. Sarah Kane committed suicide four years later, as we prepared to build the shell of the Rose. Harold Pinter was one of the few who recognised her genius: 'It was a very startling and tender voice, but she was appalled by the world in which she lived and the world within herself', he said. Pinter provided a highlight of the year for me with the return of Julie Christie to the stage in his *Old Times* with Harriet Walter and Leigh Lawson at Wyndhams.

Our Lottery application would be driven by the Trust; Geoff Howard, as the professional expert, would lead the application. In addition to the phenomenon of the National Lottery, there had been other funding changes since 1989: Greater London Arts was replaced by the London Arts Board; the Arts Council of England had been established the previous year when the Arts Council of Great Britain was split into three separate bodies; the Arts Council's National Lottery Fund had been established. This last detail was evidently momentous at national level, of course. As far as Kingston was concerned and despite the excitement of the chase, on reflection the quest for funding from the National Lottery acted as no more than an interesting diversion which, neither then nor now, amounted to anything very much.

However, there were consequences. The first impact which the Lottery had was to allow RBK quietly to remove the commitment made six years before to fund very fully the capital cost of the theatre. When advance notice was given of a Lottery application, the estimated cost of the building had risen to £8 million, and the application was for £5.5 million. 'Other sources of funding' indicated that St. George PLC would provide £2 million (the 'planning gain': building the shell) and Royal Borough of Kingston £500,000 – a saving of £4 million on the original commitment. In addition, and in anticipation of a successful application, the Trust's Appeal Committee began to make plans to raise £1 million, plans which were reliant upon a successful bid, but could not be set in motion until the Lottery outcome was known. Had the application been successful, all may have been well – although we would have built a theatre rather different from the one we now have.

In fact, we were in difficulties from another quarter. It was John Major's government which created the National Lottery by Statute in 1994. Quick from the blocks was the Royal Opera House with an ambitious programme of redevelopment and expansion which led, as early as the Summer of 1995, to an award of £55 million with a potential £23.5 million to follow. Such vast sums being distributed to one project in London and the insouciant words of Grey Gowrie, chairman of the Arts Council of England, might have given us a false sense of security: 'The world of the arts', said Gowrie, 'can rest assured that this award is in no way "crowding out" other projects … of a regional or national character. It will not affect the great number of community and amateur awards we are making'. However, the public outcry from the regions was swift and understandable; it quickly became clear that other projects inside the M25 would have to fight rather harder for sympathetic notice.

As we began to move forward, we hit another rock. The Education and Leisure Services Committee resolved that further funding for KTT to cover short-term development of the project should be identified through a 'loan mechanism'. As if one own goal was not enough, within minutes of the whistle being blown to begin the Lottery game, a second came as the result of a political *volte-face*. The Committee announced that there was a need to consider long-term revenue funding implications for a completed theatre and that 'under current Council budgetary restraints, it is unlikely revenue funding would be made available'. Was this a calculated move to sink the theatre project or was it political ineptness? What was clear was that, in announcing its intention in these terms, the politicians were effectively strangling the only viable alternative source of funding – the National Lottery. It was inconceivable that the Arts Council would recommend financing a project which was apparently intent on milking the Lottery as a cash cow, whilst taking no financial responsibility itself.

David Jacobs, who as Chairman had received this particular face-slap in a letter from the Head of Secretariat, was particularly taken aback and wrote to his board that he was 'shattered to receive news of this change in the position of the Local Authority who up until this time had consistently supported the theatre'. It would be an understatement to suggest that the original trustees were a little indignant at the suggestion that they should go elsewhere to find funding: they had been giving their time for six years at the instigation of RBK and with an assurance both of capital and revenue funding, recognised in the 1989 budget and subsequently year by year. As they gathered for the board meeting on 13th November 1995, the mood was angry.

David Jacobs opened the meeting, saying that he had only learned of the decision when the Surrey Comet had contacted him for a comment: he had naturally been dumb-founded particularly as he recalled the Leader of the Council speaking a few months previously at the 'Kingston Matters' forum saying how important the creation of a new theatre would be for the future of Kingston. Robin Hutchinson echoed Jacobs' dismay, but asked that Ian Reid be given the opportunity to present the Authority's view, as so far the only information to date had come from the media reporting the Education Committee's meeting. Councillor Reid, an RBK appointed Trustee, as well as being a member of the majority Liberal Democrat party, was also the Chairman of the Education and Leisure Committee and so had presided over its decision. His was not a convincing response: it was the majority feeling within the administration, he said, that while they would like to see a theatre they could not commit to revenue funding of 'several thousand pounds per year'. He expressed the wish 'to explore all avenues of revenue funding', but should KTT 'fail to make up for the absence of revenue funding from RBK, at that stage KTT would be able to go back to RBK and ask them to re-consider the issue'. It was not an impressive presentation, but it fuelled the anger and led to a sustained and coherent debate which, in the aftermath, gave pause for thought in other quarters. Tony Anstee referred to the unique quality of the opportunity that existed to provide a theatre, and pointed out its place in the broader Charter Quay development, a significant project at a particular historical moment. 'It is not common these days for enthusiastic, competent developers to engage upon a project such as Charter Quay', he said. What, he asked would happen 'should the issue of the theatre lead to the demise of the development?' Jim Daly reminded the meeting that the theatre project and the establishment of Kingston Theatre Trust had been initiatives of RBK and had enjoyed all party support, so there had been no political differences, and it was 'clearly understood that the capital commitment would have revenue implications'. Daly knew what he was talking about: he had been the Chairman of the Policy and Resources committee at the time and, calculating that the theatre revenue would have required something between a 1p and 2p rate (a 1p rate represented approximately £250,000) he 'had been most concerned to make it crystal clear that the capital commitment carried with it a known revenue effect'. Ivan Hannaford gave the discussion further historical context, referring to the 1986 Working Party and the popular desire for a theatre. David Jacobs spoke of 'the unanimous view on the benefits the theatre would bring to the local economy', which had been expressed in the Kingston Matters forum and voiced by the current Leader of the Council. Keith Grant, the University trustee, 'shared the sense of desolation that had been expressed by fellow Directors'.

The Board rejected the proposal of the Council that a loan mechanism be created to keep the Trust going on the grounds that it would be inappropriate, but also it would represent an unwelcome reinforcement of what appeared to be a damaging change of relationship between the local authority and KTT. They determined to meet with the Leader of the Council as a matter of urgency, not least to understand from him how he envisaged a business plan might be developed, particularly in the light of the impending National Lottery application. I thought that it was beginning to feel like playing tennis with a cricket bat on a hillside.

In a letter to the Leader of the Council the following day, David Jacobs wrote that 'the issue is the future of Kingston as a town', and that his Board felt 'shock, upset and abject dismay'. Hardly surprising! Only a few months before, this very same leader had been talking about the theatre as a long-term investment for the Borough: was this what his long-term vision amounted to?

At the same time, as the Council's decision was in the public domain, a statement to the press was released which simply stated, 'The Kingston Theatre Trust, which was set up at the behest of the Council, is determined that the unique opportunity presented by the Charter Quay development to provide a theatre for Kingston upon Thames' residents shall not be squandered'. The communiqué went on to say that the Trust would seek to 're-establish the cross party support that gave birth to the theatre proposals in 1989 and has been the cornerstone of developments since that time'.

The immediate result was an attempt at remedial work on the part of the ruling group, with John Tilley agreeing to attend a hastily convened meeting on 4th December 1995. It was evident that Tilley was rather taken aback at the response of KTT, but also he had not appreciated the ramifications of his administration's recent decisions. There had been serious political misjudgments and it now appeared that he was at pains to calm the waters. Rightly so: the whole project had been put in jeopardy, with a danger that the developers might lose confidence and the Lottery application might fall at the first hurdle. Peter Winfield kept a detailed note of the meeting and wrote, with his customary deadpan irony, that 'we had misunderstood the position in respect of the Council withdrawing its financial support'. Further, Tilley had had 'conversations with a sponsor whom he was not prepared to name, but the suggestion was that they would consider contributing £100,000/ £150,000 per annum towards the cost of the theatre'. This was an interesting bolt to change the mood from blue. However, Tilley was 'unable to answer questions about what strings might be attached to the proposal he had mooted'. This small detail could, of course, be crucial in preserving the integrity of the artistic policy.

Tilley did want closer links with KTT to avoid the Trust getting into what he called 'hypothetical corners' leading to 'megaphone diplomacy' – presumably a reference to our press statement.

The 4th December meeting agreed to the setting up of an 'Action Group' from the ruling Liberal Democrat party, RBK officers and the Theatre Trust. But suspicion and uncertainty prevailed. It was to be another two years before all three political parties on the Council engaged in concerted all-party agreement and action with the Trust. This was preceded by the almost inevitable failure of the Lottery application.

The Action Group at least offered an opportunity to steady things and, not least, to avoid the disintegration of the Trust: there was a danger that individuals would decide that enough was enough, and the frustrations were becoming too deep. I proposed that Peter Winfield should represent the Trust along with Tony Anstee and Robin Hutchinson. I was keen that Hutchinson should be kept on board: he was becoming particularly irritated and, as Winfield records, 'this ropes in Robin and I thought it was an astute move'. Winfield had for many years worked to keep Mark Gilks, the Director of Planning, on side as far as the theatre was concerned. At this meeting he 'found Mark Gilks' performance disappointing' with a 'lack of material facts'. His letter, with its implication of distrust for the planning officer and scepticism about the potential for a satisfactory Lottery application, concludes with a suggestion of what the Trust should now focus on: its 'prime objective is to get a freehold site allocated for the theatre, the shell to be provided by St. George, the Council to make a capital contribution towards the fitting out, and to re-affirm its policy to support the running costs of the theatre less the amount that might be forthcoming from sponsors'. Winfield had always been seen as the Chairman of the Appeals Committee, when the time came. Knowing what his own weighty responsibility should be in the years ahead, he said: 'the Theatre Trust will be responsible for launching an appeal in due course to provide funds to finish and furnish the theatre', and he concluded that 'it will be concerned with making appointments to ensure the future running of the theatre, to protect artistic integrity, and generally to ensure that the theatre is launched on prudent and acceptable lines'.

The first Action Group meeting took place early in the new year of 1996 and there were expressions of goodwill from all sides and a determination to keep the theatre project – and the whole Charter Quay development – on the rails. In trying to identify alternative funding, the Leader of the Council reiterated that he knew of a potential sponsor, although could not as yet reveal the identity. It never fully became clear who this was, although overtures to the Bovis Group were rebuffed during succeeding months. Notable at this meeting were the interventions of the new Chief executive of RBK, Bernard Quoroll, who announced his intention to set up an RBK Project Team of officers at the highest level. Not since the departure of Robert McCloy had the Chief Executive played anything more than a passive role in the theatre. Quoroll would he said, amongst other things, play a direct role in the National Lottery application. Geoff Howard was surprised, but declared himself willing to surrender responsibility for the Lottery if minimising costs to the local authority in terms of his external consultancy time was so important. Both Peter Winfield and I were to express serious reservations about this in the coming weeks, and the Trust took the view that Howard's involvement was vital. Generally, though, the meeting seemed to be an affirmation of commitment by RBK to the theatre, and we initially took the view that for the new Chief Executive to play a central role was positive. This view did not solidify into substantial confidence as time went on and as Quoroll revealed the extent of his capabilities.

By the time the Board met three weeks later reservations began to emerge. Peter Winfield reported on the positive aspects of the two meetings that had been held since the last unhappy Board in November. However, he was concerned about a lack of action in the intervening weeks. Privately, he was worried about a perceived gap between three parties – RBK, St. George and the Prudential – as to what amount ought to be made available for RBK's land interest against the background of the developer being required to provide the shell of the theatre. It appeared that possibly as much as £1 million was missing to secure the site of the theatre and the shell of the building. Winfield, who had an array of professional contacts, based his assessment on conversations he had had on his own initiative. He made his assessment known following a question

I asked of Mark Gilks and of Ian Reid at the 22nd January meeting. It was a simple question, although there was an obvious subtext: 'Once the 106 Agreement is in place, will the shell of the theatre be built?' Mark Gilks replied unequivocally that this would be the case. He further affirmed that the developers would provide the shell free of charge, a constant factor over the years. However, Reid's response was more equivocal: with a number of different parties involved in the development, he said, different perspectives might need to be accommodated. Was the ground shifting again? Winfield felt that St. George was genuinely committed to the whole development including the theatre. The Friend's Provident issue had still not been resolved, but if necessary a compulsory purchase order could secure that – an order which the local authority would have to effect: it would be a classic example of the use of a compulsory purchase order. So was there a problem? Reid saw the project moving forward on twin tracks as far as the theatre was concerned: 'On the one hand development project activity involving RBK personnel with KTT input, and on the other hand work targeting National Lottery funding and partnership revenue possibilities'. Alarmingly, the new Chief Executive of RBK had designated himself driver of both these trains.

Bernard Quoroll had taken up residence in the Guildhall late in 1995. His was not an auspicious appointment; in the short time he remained in Kingston he never grasped the theatre issue, though he did try to juggle with it. He saw that the theatre was causing consternation, not least amongst his political masters and they saw him as the man to lead for RBK: Tilley had concluded a New Year message in early 1996 that he would ask 'Bernard [Quoroll] and Mark [Gilks] to progress things from the Council's end'.

Quoroll's stay in Kingston was brief and undistinguished, until he moved on to the Isle of Wight where headaches were caused, before the islanders were able to cut short his tenure on the grounds that he apparently lost the confidence of the island's ruling group. While he was in Kingston, he gave the impression of wanting to be 'hands on'. I recall conversations with him about Lottery funding – we went together to the offices of the London Arts Board on 18th June 1996 – when his declared strategy was to 'tick here, and tack there'. I never got to the bottom of what he meant, and I suspect neither did he.

Perhaps the following was an example of Quoroll's ticking and tacking: it is clear from council documents that some in the authority wanted ownership of a project which had the potential to be prestigious, irrespective of their understanding. In a briefing paper to the new Director of Education the following note was made in mid-1996 (a few months after Quoroll's arrival): 'Chief Exec. keen to restore the balance between RBK and KTT on managing the project. It can be argued that KTT has been allowed to take over the reins to an inappropriate extent, contributing to a perception on the part of some Councillors that the theatre project is "theirs" – ie. KTT's – not "ours", whereas KTT was established by RBK originally to assist the Council in realising the theatre'. This travesty of what was actually happening is perhaps indicative of why little was achieved during his curtailed tenure, other than a series of awkward situations. The document goes on to say that 'the establishment of a more effective partnership between the two parties is thus critical to the project's success, best achieved perhaps by close liaison between KTT's Action Group and RBK's officer group'.

It demonstrates a fundamental misunderstanding: the Action Group was in fact created to comprise members of both KTT and RBK. By the end of March, KTT had been asking for further meetings. A meeting in May was cancelled at the last minute and a gathering in early June became a 'briefing meeting' in which Quoroll, Gilks and the newly appointed Director of Education John Braithwaite, gave their perspective on developments prior to a KTT board meeting later in the day.

However, there were some positive developments in mid-1996. The argument about High Street presence seemed to have been won, with the re-orientation of the theatre in RHWL's designs. The siting of the proposed theatre building had also been altered, to approximately where the current Rose stands. However, the intention was still to cover the Hogs Mill, although now with a piazza rather than the entrance to the theatre. This would become one of the difficulties at the planning stage. At the same meeting at which this and its implications were discussed, the departure of the Director of Planning, Mark Gilks, was announced.

His role in relation to KTT would be taken by the Acting Director of Environmental Services, Alan McMillan, a transition which was not entirely untroubled.

Amongst concerns about the new design plans, was that the theatre would now be built in the final phase. Questioning of officers made it clear that plans for financial partnerships were as vague as when first proposed by the Council. The University, for instance, remained elusive although their Vice Chancellor was soon to retire which held out hope for some change in the future. The only other feasible contact seemed to be the Gateway School of Recording and Music Technology which was then based on a University campus at Kingston Hill. If this was the answer to the funding crisis, it was inauspicious. At this meeting it was also mooted that perhaps the Lottery process should progress in two stages.

When I accompanied Bernard Quoroll, along with Colin Bloxham, to the London Arts Board in June we met with John Kieffer and Joyce Wilson. They were clear in their advice and the principal points gave good food for thought. Kieffer saw the University as a very important element, both for its influence and also because of an inherent strength in artistic and educational partnerships. So there was work to be done there. He warned, however, about partnerships with the likes of Gateway, which might have financial clout, but equally might try to use this to drive its own commercial interests and such ties might taint a lottery bid: we'd have to 'tick' and then 'tack' our way around that one, Mr. Quorroll! Kieffer strongly recommended that a resident company should be a central part of planning. He also stressed the value of adaptability within the space. Really, it reinforced the sense that we needed to create something special and distinctive, which might mean that we should not merely identify a resident company, but create one.

However, the RBK/KTT relationship had worsened: communication became difficult to a point which led David Jacobs to write a second letter to John Tilley, in November 1996, almost exactly a year after his first. The particular provocation was the behaviour of one senior officer who had formed the view that 'there was no need to consult with the Trust prior to design proposals passing into the public domain'. Alan McMillan, by then confirmed as Director of Environmental Services, had announced to the KTT Board on 28th November that he had submitted a planning application for registration. There had been no communication on this with the Trust since June and certainly no discussion with regard, for instance, to the London Arts Board visit and its implications on the planning issue. Various channels were available, either individually, through the Building Sub-committee and through the Action Group, but none had been taken and despite requests the Action Group had not met for months. Peter Winfield voiced the Trust's dismay: the Leader of the Council had said clearly that the way forward was for a proper liaison between RBK and the Trust, yet there had been none since June. It appeared to David Jacobs that McMillan took the view that the Trust was 'part of the general public and as such would be able to register their views through the normal channels'. McMillen was asked to seek St. George's agreement to freeze the registration process of the application until proper vetting by the Trust could take place, which he very reluctantly did. With his tail between his legs, McMillan invited the members of the Building Sub-committee to his office in December. Sadly, this was not the end of *his* ticking and tacking.

The proposal to include the theatre in only the final phase remained, and this would mean that the shell would not be completed for between three and four years. Given the history of market downturns, we were really concerned that to have the theatre in the final stage offered the potential for default on the part of the builder. At an Action Group meeting in early January, with Peter Winfield leading for the Trust, McMillen suggested that the developers could not be expected to start the shell of the building without the fitting out money in place. This was either an ill-thought-out suggestion or it was deliberately provocative: the developer had a legal obligation to produce the shell and Peter Winfield was terse and direct in saying that they should get on with it speedily. Winfield was clear that the project needed much more detail and substance before we could begin asking for money. No fundraising appeal would be successful if any uncertainty affected the project. In retrospect, I suppose that McMillen was given the same briefing note from the Chief Executive that was given to the new Director of Education in June 1996. Our nervousness over the reliability of council officers was reinforced when Quoroll himself announced that he felt that RBK was in a weak negotiating position with regard to the theatre. Yet again, Winfield had to counsel the need for a positive and proactive approach. Little did anyone know at that moment, and it is one of the ironies in the story, that to be included as a part of the final stage of the development would work to the advantage of the theatre in terms of its final realisation.

The New Year brought the moment of the signing of the S106 agreement – in this case between RBK and the developer St George, with the Kingston Theatre Trust as an active partner. It should have been a moment of celebration as the finalising of the agreement for the planning to go ahead, whilst securing from the developer their contribution to the community: in this case, the shell of the theatre. The planning application was submitted in January 1997, which meant the time was ripe to publicise the agreement fully. It was agreed that each of the three parties, RBK, St George and Kingston Theatre Trust, should issue their individual press releases on the same day. However, it would be important that these be in harmony and so a meeting was set to compare notes. The meeting was convened in Bernard Quoroll's office. Each party ran through their intended press releases. RBK's contained the detail of the S106 and the ensuing benefits to Kingston. Quoroll described the RBK release as 'playing out the facts familiar to everyone' with regard to the provision of the shell of Kingston's long-awaited theatre. However, Geoff Howard immediately noticed the detail in black and white which had worried the Trust during the previous year: the agreement to be publicised now provided for St George's to give a sum of money to RBK for 'community facilities' in the event that the theatre was not built. Howard challenged this inclusion as the whole of the project had been predicated on the provision of the shell of a theatre from a planning gain. Quoroll argued that there was no intention of invoking the cash provision, but it had to be there for legal reasons to cover all eventualities. The Trust insisted that this so-called legal requirement be reviewed. Our celebrations were inevitably muted and we remained guarded.

The Trust determined to move quickly: we would attempt to raise the bulk of capital expenditure to complete and equip the theatre from a Lottery application whilst recognising that there would certainly be a £1 million shortfall which would become the object of an appeal, to be led by Peter Winfield.

A Lottery application for Phase One funding to test the viability of the project and in particular develop a coherent business plan began in earnest. Of course, it was shaped under the cloud of uncertainty provoked by the Council's wavering on funding commitments. Arts Business Limited was asked in early 1997 by RBK, who of course held the purse strings, to complete a feasibility study. A steering group, which included Robin Hutchinson, Geoff Howard and me from the Trust, was set up to take the application forward. It was anticipated that this would be presented in June 1997 and, if successful, a further application would be made the following year for design development. Another member of the Steering Group was Colin Bloxham. Bloxham, sometimes in the face of unnecessary difficulties, always worked tirelessly in the interests of what would become Kingston's Rose. He was happy to take anyone to task: when ABL wrote that 'we should not appear too ambitious at this stage', Bloxham's response was that it 'is vital to get this message across at every opportunity – the Kingston Theatre will have national, even international relevance', echoing the ambition which Robin Hutchinson and I had always harboured for Kingston.

In the context of the difficulties of the Trust's dealings with some in the Guildhall, this was pie in the sky! Tensions persisted. McMillen continued to appear obtuse at the Trust's February meeting, insisting yet again that it was his understanding that the construction of the shell should not commence until the funding to fit out the theatre was in place. It was affirmed several times that McMillen's understanding was wrong, although it did not seem to worry him. And then, in an extraordinary intervention, Ian Reid suggested that the Trust should change its objective and consider an arts centre on the site instead of a 550 seat theatre. What was going on behind closed doors in the Guildhall? Was Reid behaving as a sort of 'stalking horse'? Were forces moving to halt the whole process? Would the Council consider a one-off payment from St. George in place of the theatre shell? We all became increasingly wary. Of one thing we were sure: the project was as uncertain as it had ever been, but without either clear or valid reason. For a hardcore group of us on the Trust such apparent slaps in the face made us even more doggedly determined. We also learned from the experiences and found support in the different strengths that we had. Robin Hutchinson became more pro-active behind the scenes and did not rely on the RBK bridge with the developers: he went directly to them. Peter Winfield brought all his diplomacy, skill, wit and knowledge to the table to keep the mandarins up to the mark. David Jacobs would not be diverted and even from time to time removed the metaphorical gloves in confrontation, showing qualities which were probably never associated in the public eye with Jacobs the urbane broadcaster.

When the Royal Fine Art Commission, on behalf of Hampton Court Palace, lodged a planning objection on the grounds of the height and bulk of the design for the whole site, we were exasperated – though not at the RFAC. McMillen had not engaged the Trust effectively in the development of the planning application in the first place. Later, he had made light of the objections when he first reported them to the Action Group in March and suggested 'no fundamental changes were anticipated' and he was 'optimistic about receiving support from the Royal Fine Art Commission'. Bland words for the sake of what? In a letter to Kingston Council, the secretary of the RFAC wrote that 'the housing element of the scheme as presented [is] fundamentally flawed and totally unacceptable'.

Three weeks later, Peter Winfield expressed his dismay that the Action Group had been led to believe that the RFAC was looking for 'minor tweaks rather than major revision' and so he concluded in his understated way that, 'the situation could represent a setback'. The reduction of mass could reduce the economic viability of the overall scheme to the point at which it became impractical for St George to continue. They had only entered into an agreement to provide the shell of the theatre as a planning gain from which they would benefit: the development must pay for the theatre. In addition, detailed objections had been made to the height of the development. The theatre design at that time included a fly tower and its height was now a problem. Geoff Howard wrote to Robin Derham in June, expressing the Trust's concern about this, but did not receive a reply, and so the question of the fly tower design was left to play its significant but surprising part in future developments in the years ahead, even though it would never be built.

And why did Derham not reply? Amongst the 'minor tweaks' which were effected was a parting of the ways between the developer, St George, and the architects, RHWL. They had arrived at what Debbie Applin of St. George described as 'something of an impasse'. St. George had moved quickly and appointed John Thompson & Partners, who met with members of the Trust in July to present what was described as 'the new scheme'. With a degree of pragmatism which we came to associate more and more with St. George in the coming years, they said that they were very happy should the Trust want to continue to work with RHWL on the theatre.

The new plans in outline affected the theatre probably in relation to the fly tower, but as yet that was not resolved. In other ways it impacted only insofar as its relationship with the piazza was now less strong, but the architects would focus on the theatre/ piazza relationship as being of major concern. Its orientation remained in the position it had been revised to the previous year, and as the current Rose now stands.

Elsewhere, not too far distant, the Peter Hall Company was installed at the Old Vic theatre. Hall was experimenting with seasons of repertory theatre, including new plays and classics, in which each play would use more or less the same design and therefore save considerable costs. The 1997 season was of interest to me particularly owing to two of the productions. Harley Granville Barker's *Waste*, a play about a politician's fall from grace, featured a cast including Anna Carteret, Felicity Kendall, Michael Pennington and David Yelland, whose daughter Hannah was to make an important contribution to a discussion about the Rose a few years later. Granville Barker had, with his friends George Bernard Shaw and William Archer, argued for a National Theatre in the early years of the twentieth century, an ambition finally realised three quarters of a century later, under the leadership of Peter Hall. We hoped that in Kingston we would not have to wait quite so long. The other production in this season which took my personal attention was Roy MacGregor's play *Snake in the Grass*, with Sheila Reid and Greg Hicks in the cast alongside my brother, Kevin Whately, making a second foray from the small screen onto a national stage within a year. The Summer before he had been seen in an acclaimed production of *Twelve Angry Men*, directed by Harold Pinter, at the Comedy Theatre, later to become the Pinter Theatre. The cast of *Twelve Angry Men* had also included Timothy West who, a few years later, would both play at the Rose and become President of the Rose Theatre Friends.

On the political front 1997 saw changes. The General Election, which brought nineteen years of Conservative government to an end, also saw the election in Kingston of the Liberal Democrat Ed Davey. The political complexion of Kingston had begun to change some years earlier: the brief coalition of Liberals/ SDP and Labour in 1986 had seen the setting up of the Arts Working Party, which had in turn led to the creation of the Kingston Theatre Trust under a succeeding Conservative administration. The balance of power then began to swing between the Conservatives and the Liberal Democrats, with the latter gradually gaining the ascendancy. Davey's first election victory was probably aided by the intervention of James Goldsmith, who took some Conservative votes, but thereafter Davey was returned on his own account. A committed constituency MP, he quickly expressed his support for the theatre, seeing it as important in the commercial and cultural development of Kingston. Also in 1997, Derek Osbourne became the Leader of the Council for the first time, in succession to John Tilley. Osbourne had been a member of KTT as a political party representative, although his largely invisible involvement in that capacity gave no hint of the role he was to play in the years to come.

There were some political difficulties. The Conservative group had voted against the revised Planning Application. One of their number, Councillor Jane Smith, was also a member of the Trust. She explained to the Trust's October meeting that her party had no objection to the theatre, but had concerns about other aspects of the development. The Labour group had abstained on the grounds that there were aspects of the scheme that they did not like and, while they supported the theatre, they were not confident the scheme would deliver the theatre, particularly now there was no longer any provision within RBK to finance it in future years. The Secretary of State for the Environment, who happened also to be John Prescott, the Deputy Prime Minister, intervened on the planning question, placing an embargo on RBK formally issuing approval while he decided whether it should be called in. This would in all likelihood lead to a public enquiry. The reasons given related to concerns expressed by English Heritage and by our neighbouring Richmond Borough Council, rather than political actions from within Kingston. David Jacobs swiftly wrote to the Secretary of State to press the Trust's case. In the full knowledge of this Lorraine Monk, a Theatre Trustee, as a Labour Councillor, was then party to another letter to Prescott, this time from the Labour group, asking him to 'call in' the application, an action which could conceivably compromise the development to the point where the theatre project would become unviable. It was an interesting situation: as a trustee she had a legal obligation to represent the best interests of the Trust. However, events prevented the issue developing.

By the end of the year, the planning impasse had eased with English Heritage withdrawing their objections, subject to some manageable conditions. The Secretary of State had not as yet withdrawn the planning embargo, but there was hope this would happen early in the new year and by the end of February 1998 the green light began to flicker on.

Meanwhile, there continued to be problems between the Guildhall and the Trust. David Jacobs had to write what seemed now to be an annual letter of concern to the Leader of the Council. This time it was over the detail of the S106 Agreement, the crucial factor in the contract by which the developer would build the shell of the theatre as a planning gain. At the October Board meeting the Trust asked to see, in confidence, the full agreement prior to its signing, but the Director of Environmental Services, Alan McMillen, demurred despite this very point being discussed and tacitly agreed on countless occasions. Yet again, a tiresome and unnecessary barrier had to be dismantled in order to ensure that no irreparable blunder be made. The Leader of the Council saw no problem with the Board's request and instructed McMillen to ensure it happened. And a good job that this was done, too: the brief from RBK to the solicitors drawing up the S106 agreement was anything but clear in the context of the theatre interest: the Trust had to ask for a categorical assurance that the agreement would make clear that St George would have to provide the freehold site for the theatre and that they would build the shell in accordance with agreed plans and specification.

In its efforts to ensure that the theatre would neither at best be a side-show, nor at worst wither and die, the Trust had decided to redouble efforts to keep its profile high. Yet again, Robin Hutchinson came to the fore in developing what he called a 'Profile Plan' which would keep the theatre in the public mind, but would also develop the arguments for its central place in Kingston's future both as a major artistic venue in the region and as a significant contributor to commercial development. Meetings were planned with all the major council committees with a view to ensuring that everyone in the political process would be clear about the Trust's plans. We were also at pains to marginalise the attempts being made in some quarters to resurrect the ghostly arts centre.

At the very time we were developing the Lottery application and insisting to ABL that the application should be 'beefed up' in terms of our ambitions, we did not want that particular spectre to walk the corridors of power and attract the press. With the uncertainty caused by RHWL's departure from the main scheme and the ambiguity of St. George's suggestion that we could retain them for the theatre, I suggested that we urge St. George to take on a theatre consultant for expert guidance and I suggested that the best individual to do this would be Iain Macintosh of Theatre Projects. Whilst Theatre Projects did eventually tender for the work, it was clear that Macintosh would not be available. Carr & Angier were eventually appointed.

We still had to ensure that the Lottery was not seen as the 'do or die' factor, given the uncertainty of outcome. The discussion of timetables with the Director of Environmental Services frequently turned to his caveat about the need for funding from the Lottery – a phenomenon that had emerged on the national scene years after Kingston had made its commitment to building a theatre.

The Lottery application was finally turned down at the end of March 1998. To most of us it did not come as a great surprise. For the past few years there had been public muttering about capital projects being favoured in the south-east and particularly in London. The grant of £78.5 million to the Royal Opera House developments had fanned the flames of furore in other parts of the country and so Kingston's position inside the M25 almost certainly undermined the application. London Arts Board met with us to explain that while the project scored highly in most regards, only projects which would demonstrably contribute to local, regional and national strategies and which already had an effective track record at this time stood any chance.

While some were bitterly disappointed and thought that this was probably the last throw of the dice, a hard core – as ever urged on by the optimism of David Jacobs – saw this as an opportunity. As long as the shell was delivered we could continue to move forward. We began to explore how we might make a virtue of the shell and develop what we described as the 'Warehouse Theatre Concept'. Each of us had different notions as to what this might mean, but it would eventually lead to some new and radical thinking. Provided we could keep all sides moving forward, the Trust had the chance of transforming the project.

There were three particular uncertainties. Firstly, in May a new political administration was ushered in, the Conservatives having won power at the local elections. Their leader, David Edwards, assured us that they would continue to support the theatre and particularly the building of the shell. However, here lay the second problem: difficulties had developed as the terms of the S106 agreement were being thrashed out: St George valued the proposed shell at £1.7 million, whereas the RBK estimate was £2.3million. The lower figure would be the one that St. George would offer as a cash settlement, should the theatre building be cancelled.

For many of us, it was the third that was of most concern: Peter Winfield became ill. At the moment when we were about to move towards a public appeal, the wise and witty man who had been waiting for nearly a decade to lead the campaign for funds became seriously incapacitated.

9
Finding the Rose

A second experience with a production at the Swan Theatre, Stratford helped focus my mind at just the right moment. In early 1996 I had begun work with Jeremy James Taylor creating a new production of *The Beggar's Opera* for the National Youth Music Theatre. Jeremy had persuaded Martin Best to let us use his brilliant but unpublished arrangement for two guitars, double bass and percussion and we had recruited Mark Ashford to lead the musicians. Mark had recently won the BBC Radio 2 Young Musician of the Year and his touch and lyrical skill was thrilling. On our way to Edinburgh , we opened at the Brewery Arts in Kendall and four weeks later had played to full houses at the George Square Theatre in Edinburgh, winning the BBC Radio 3 award for best production. The following year, in the Autumn of 1997, with a strong cast which included Madeleine Worrall as Polly Peacham, Christian Coulson as Macheath, Lucy-Anne Bradshaw as Lucy Lockitt, Neil Clench as Lockitt, Barty Lee as Peacham, Joanna Hewitt as Mrs Peacham and Oliver Thornton as Filch, a week at the Lyric Hammersmith preceded a return to the Swan Theatre, Stratford.

Trevor Nunn had forged ahead in the late nineteen eighties with the building of the Swan despite warnings from the official bureaucracies (the Arts Council and the Arts Ministry) that the move was unwise. He wrote a little later that 'the Swan is not the first and we must all pray, not the last national treasure to come into being against the wishes of officialdom'. The Swan was not created to replace a theatre, nor to give an alternative space for the work the RSC was already doing. It was designed to allow them to explore the work of Shakespeare's contemporaries on a stage which would offer every opportunity to reveal a rich and, to some degree, lost repertoire.

That this has met with so much success is to do in large measure with the theatre architecture. Speaking on the occasion of the RSC's fiftieth anniversary in August 2011 Gregory Doran said that the Swan's success stemmed considerably from the quality of Michael Reardon's design, described in *The Observer* as an 'exceptionally attractive performance space ... first impressions are of precision, harmony, versatility, joy'.

Working for a second time in this space served to reinforce my sense that theatres which drew their influence architecturally from an age when drama was at its most popular were particularly exciting. The Swan, of course, is not a realisation of an older theatre, but in the actor-audience relationship it reflects something of what we know about Elizabethan public performance spaces. William Poel in the Nineteenth Century and later Tyrone Guthrie in the Twentieth wanted to explore this. Peter Brook had written in simple but revelatory terms about the future of good theatre being in *The Empty Space*, which the public theatres of Shakespeare's times essentially were. Whatever Sam Wanamaker's motives were in his crusade to rebuild the Globe, the audiences found and still find an energy of their own there as participants in theatrical performance. My brilliant young National Youth Music Theatre actors, many of them now successful professionals, at the Swan found playing the space exciting and stimulating because of the engagement with the audiences in an intimate place which paradoxically allowed for expansive gesture – and a break from the increasingly prohibitive shackles of naturalism. That's not to say that it is an easy space for actors: it's not, but it does offer great rewards for both players and the punters. The phenomenon of television has developed to the point where night after night people can watch what is often effective dramatic realism oozed through the tube into their living rooms, as they sink placidly into their sofas. Good theatre would not survive if it merely tried to ape what anyone could see on the television. The Elizabethan and Jacobean theatre spaces were essentially interactive and some of our new theatres and companies were beginning to hark back to this past time in gaining inspiration for theatre architecture and space.

This is not to suggest that such spaces work only for classical text. Some of our own contemporary innovative companies, like Complicité and Frantic Assembly, have flourished in spaces without the constriction of the proscenium. Crucially both actors and audiences began to be stimulated by them. I came back from Stratford with a sense that we could capitalise on an opportunity in Kingston. In all the debates and delays and also the developing sense that we should have a theatre that would be more than a local theatre, we had nevertheless allowed other forces to weigh us down. Going all the way back to the 1986 Working Party, we had been compromising in an effort to keep all the forces on side, arguing to keep the idea of a theatre in Kingston afloat, without really clearly defining what that theatre should be. As long as we got the theatre, was the inherent assumption, it could be adapted to suit a variety of possibly conflicting demands, provided that it had enough flexibility.

In retrospect, the failure of our Lottery application gave us an opportunity. Indeed, it was an occasion that, oddly, elicited only the briefest disappointment. Robin Hutchinson and Geoff Howard began to talk about a 'Warehouse Theatre' which was a shorthand term for making the best of the shell that the developers were bound to provide and at the same time heading off any moves to accept a pay-off instead of the shell. I began to think about how that might allow us to create a more attractive and effective space. Within the simplicity of our shell, could we create something of the impact that the Swan Theatre has? The Swan had, after all, been built in another shell – the shell of the old Conference Hall (which was in fact the very original Memorial Theatre of 1879). The S106 Agreement was still being negotiated and, owing to the changing situation, a detail was included which would allow for the specification of the shell to change, should that be necessary prior to building work beginning.

There was still a danger that the Council might take the cash option, but Robin Hutchinson's work with a profile plan and the speedy and up-beat response to the Lottery rejection allowed us to keep the initiative. It also became evident that were a cash payment to be made it could not be diverted into other concerns: it would have to be spent on the arts, which was obviously to our advantage. There were still rumblings about reconsidering the whole project and substituting an arts centre if not taking money in lieu. However, there was a significant boost in July 1998 when the Council agreed that the cash option would not be included in the S106 agreement and that the building of the shell was non-negotiable. Perish the thought that this might have had something to do with the fact that RBK had valued the shell at £2.3 million and St. George was adamant that they would not offer anything more than £1.7 million as a cash sum!

There was now a climate of renewed energy with all three political parties and the officers of the borough working in a more effective harmony with the Trust than heretofore. Almost inevitably this was the result of particular personalities. For the Liberal Democrats, Derek Osbourne and then Roger Hayes were clear in their commitment. Kevin Davis became Conservative leader and engaged with enthusiasm. Ed Naylor offered Labour support with a down-to-earth and practical good sense. Meanwhile, John Braithwaite, now settled in as Director of Education, became the leading council officer in the project and Colin Bloxham no longer found himself ploughing a lonely furrow. Braithwaite's unfussy and sensible counsel and clear personal determination was of enormous value. He was always willing to offer himself and his office for meetings, often late into the night. He found funding for feasibility and development work in relation to the warehouse idea. John Braithwaite was to retire in 2002, having seen the shell of the theatre to completion.

The mechanism by which to harness the newly found energy was a Steering Group – later called the Feasibility Group – comprising Hayes, Davies and Naylor with Bloxham and Braithwaite from RBK and Robin Hutchinson, David Nield and me along with Geoff Howard from the Trust. We would oversee the three key areas: the building, the artistic policy and the business implications and plan, with decision-making authority. It was to prove an effective and stimulating group for a significant time and one which would finally realise the theatre. We were not constrained by a bureaucracy. At that time, there was no political gamesmanship, as the leaders of the three groups would agree a strategic approach within our group. We would often meet away from the Guildhall – in those days the Druid's Head in the Market Place was a favourite haunt. And so the Lottery snub proved a spur: Kingston would have its theatre.

The resolution of the S106 Agreement had other affects, not least that it now, apparently, made sense to bring the building of the shell forward to an earlier stage. This good news reinforced the idea that we had been right to be suspicious over the motives of some. St. George, too, became more confident, crucially saying that they would be relaxed with regard to minor changes to the theatre specification and even offering a contribution to design work should this prompt speedy agreement. The S106 Agreement was signed finally on 9th October 1998.

Robin Hutchinson now made it his business to keep all parties thinking positively. He was particularly adept at talking with the various people who seemed to have influence within St. George. His genius for publicity was now turned to their account and he persuaded the developer that the theatre should play a central part in publicising their housing development. They played the game: on one occasion Ian Dobie, managing director of St George, West London, asked me for suitable extracts from Shakespeare – up until then foreign texts to him – which he could use in speeches about the development.

This newly-established Feasibility Group was chaired by Hutchinson with characteristic gusto and with a sense of purpose always leavened by humour. Whilst Carr & Angier were advising on matters relating to the shell, we decided that we should enlist expert assistance on the business plan particularly. A number of people were interviewed and we appointed Michael Holden Associates in November 1998. Holden himself would lead the work and continued to do so for several years. He would give the project a new dynamic. His first brief was to prepare a report for a March 1999 meeting of the Education and Leisure Committee, a tight timetable.

It was evident from the outset that Holden would be pro-active and energetic in his work. He mastered the brief and its implications with speed, evaluated what had already been done and was willing to make critical observations where he saw contradictions or lack of clarity. I recall that at his interview he challenged the idea of a theatre limited to a capacity of 550 seats. For it to be economically viable, to 'wash its own face' financially, he suggested that there might need to be a more imaginative approach. He would leave no stone unturned in examining the potential already there, but he did not accept all the assumptions which had been made. For instance, he was concerned that should we open the building in some form for public work the chances of raising further significant capital funding would be weak. He did not challenge the idea of a 'warehouse' space, but was concerned that the original specification might not be the most appropriate way forward.

Shortly after his appointment he came to see me at home, which was when I first got to talk to him at length. He had been involved in a variety of ways in the design and development of many theatre spaces. He had played a significant role in the development of the Globe, first as a consultant but later for a time as Chief Executive. I had committed Tiffin School to involvement with the Globe years before. When he asked about the sort of theatre I would like to see, I talked about my experience directing in the Swan the previous year and our conversation naturally moved to discussing the archaeology of the Rose site on bankside. Perhaps we could recreate the Rose in some form.

Ostensibly, Holden's job was to help us create a business plan. However, he quickly pointed out that, without a much clearer idea of the nature of the stage and auditorium space, warehouse or whatever, this would not really be possible. He was convinced that the 550 seat mantra was misguided when there were now doubts about revenue funding, certainly not in the first instance. Estimates of the capacity of the Rose of 1587 suggest perhaps three times that number. Even allowing for the expansion of the average British bum over the English version of four hundred years ago, it would give a recreated Rose a capacity of over a thousand. It would also be relatively economic to build and have the size and adaptability which Robin Hutchinson's warehouse idea was predicated on.

There were those within our ranks who were more than merely sceptical having imagined a proscenium theatre and plush seats. John Gabb and Peter Jarvis tendered their resignations from the Trust. Others quickly adapted: David Jacobs himself took a deep breath in private, but as ever supported the steps to realise the project and in no time became as enthusiastic about the new plan as he had been for the old. John McCarthy, who had his own particular constituency within the Kingston Arts Council and the Kingston Society, expressed reservations. However, when he tendered his resignation the Chairman, in a move which took us aback, but amused us too, refused to accept it. McCarthy knew Kingston well and had been involved with the theatre campaign since his days chairing the Working Party in 1986 and, whilst not always in the van of actions, was constantly engaged and committed, asking difficult but often pertinent questions. He remained on the board for a further six months, before resigning again, this time by letter in order to brook no resistance from the chair. He continued to support the arts in Kingston and became a regular at the Rose – one of those local stalwarts who seem to have in their bloodstream concern for the cultural health of a community.

I formally proposed the idea of a theatre modeled on the Rose at the Trust meeting in March 1999. A recent public meeting had welcomed the idea of a larger space, freed from the constriction of the 550 seat stipulation. Members of the Board now asked questions as to how a larger facility could be accommodated on the site. I explained that the original Rose had a diameter of only 72 feet, making it quite compact, and so a solution might lie in that direction. Holden, meanwhile, was using a blueprint of the Rose archaeology to see how far it would fit onto the footprint of land available.

Another factor became evident: for over a year the University had had no representative on the Trust, despite our attempts to get the Vice Chancellor of the time to replace Keith Grant. Now the new Vice Chancellor, Peter Scott, grasped the significance for both the University and for Kingston. In the Feasibility Steering Group we were actively considering what the University's role might be, as Scott's Pro-Vice Chancellor Tony Mercer joined the Trust. He was quick to stress that the University would not wish to influence deliberations on design, but would be interested to see the outcome in terms of creative, academic and workshop spaces as they were considering the development of Performing Arts at the University. At that time, I little thought that I would become quite so intimately involved in *that* process. Eighteen months later, I was persuaded to leave Tiffin School, where I had taught for nearly three decades, and move across town to Kingston University and establish an undergraduate drama degree programme, before later incorporating this into and leading a new School of Performance. The idea of a theatre, influenced by the 1587 Rose, would now become bound into the developments at the University.

In the meantime, Michael Holden and I met Peter Scott and his senior management group, which included Gail Cunningham and David Miles, both of whom were to play significant roles in the years leading up to the theatre opening. Gail Cunningham would soon join the board of directors of the Trust and become David Jacobs' Vice Chair and her clear headed thinking and strategic advice came to be a crucial factor in effecting many important advances. At that first meeting in the University there was a genuine sense of an institution keen to be involved and concerned to find ways to ensure the successful development of a theatre, not only as it might benefit the University, but for the enhancement of Kingston. It was to be one of Scott's legacies as a Vice Chancellor that the University came to fulfill its civic role more fully and the focus on the theatre was the outstanding example of this.

Holden and his architect, Richard Michelmore, worked quickly. Although Holden's original task to produce an outline business plan by March 1999 was behind hand, it was for good reason: he was working up new outline plans, based on the 1587 Rose Theatre in such a way that it would fit into the footprint available in Kingston. Simultaneously, he was developing a new business plan, which could not be confirmed until the new architectural plan was accepted. It was an exciting time: at last, we were leading the game substantially, with an emerging theatre shell which could seize the imagination. By May 1999 the Rose was drawn in outline. My worries and reservations of years before of trying to create an uncertain theatre, compromised by trying to satisfy conflicting elements and forces, were now fading. The problem had been resolved in the simple idea of using a four hundred year old plan, whose discovery in 1989 had already excited the nation and its leading theatre practitioners.

One of the beauties of the original Rose was its simplicity: it was fundamentally a space with actors and audience in close proximity. Whilst our modern version would cost a little more than Henslowe's investment, it would not only be the 'First Theatre of the Twenty First Century' – our brand tag – but a bargain to boot. Ours would have the main house and also both a studio theatre and a small art gallery.

Geoff Howard had begun plans for an appeal, taking on the role he had first been commissioned for a decade earlier. The campaign was bolstered by the finessing of a situation which arose owing to the nature of theatre we were now proposing to build. We had planning permission already for a fly tower for the new theatre, but the new design would not require a fly tower. A series of late night meetings of the Feasibility Group, energised by breaks in the Druid's Head, led to an idea: we could sell the air above the theatre, in the shape of the fly tower, back to the developers which they could then develop into further accommodation. In the cold light of day, it proved not as simple as it seemed, but the plan was finally agreed and executed, which added £850,000 to the fit-out appeal.

There was one shadow: the illness of Peter Winfield. At the very moment that we could turn our attention to fundraising, the man who unquestionably had the knowledge and charisma to lead, and who had waited for nearly a decade to do so, was now struck down with the illness which would carry him off. His calm grasp of detail, his clever wit, his polite but firm handling of people who needed to be kept on task and his knowledge of where the future resources might lie were qualities we needed now more than ever before.

Only a year before Peter Winfield had become a nationally known figure in the sporting world as the breeder and owner of a great and popular racehorse, Silver Patriarch. Winfield was renowned in racing circles for his warmth and generosity, just as he was within the Trust. Silver Patriarch was pipped at the post in the 1997 Derby, having made a brilliant final dash for the line down Epsom's famous hill. It is often said that had the race been a yard or two longer Silver Patriarch would have won. But for Winfield, as he often affirmed, he raced for fun and even in his last months would travel great distances to see his beloved horse. He bravely confronted his end, helped by Silver Patriarch. He said, 'This horse gives me enormous and immeasurable pleasure. We've all got a leasehold out and I'm going to make the best of what's left for me'. Silver Patriarch did not let him down: he won a classic in that same Derby year, the St. Leger at Doncaster. The following year he returned to the Derby course to win the Coronation Cup. In a final act of generosity Winfield left his stallion to both his children and to the National Stud, so that the horse could live out a well-deserved retirement, whilst also benefiting the sport which Winfield loved. Sadly, he was not able to complete the work that he was so keen to achieve on behalf of Kingston and the theatre, but his contribution to keeping the flame alive had been immense. Peter Winfield died in November 1999.

10
Henslowe's Legacy

A routine excavation, prior to a building development on the south side of Southwark Bridge in 1989, uncovered one of the most dramatic discoveries in theatre history: the foundations of the Rose Theatre which Philip Henslowe and his partner John Cholmley had financed and which the carpenter John Griggs had built in 1587. Whilst the date of the archaeological discovery coincided with the proposal to create Kingston Theatre Trust, the new Trustees did not immediately leap to the conclusion that this might be the inspiration for Kingston's theatre: that was to happen a few years later, and was not developed without some local controversy. But for the world of theatre, the bits of chalk and brick uncovered on the corner of Rose Alley and Park Street were of monumental importance, and of a different order to the ripples being made twenty-two miles further up river.

As with so many developing projects which find their way to some sort of fulfillment and completion, a serendipity was at work as Henslowe began his theatrical speculation on the south bank of the Thames. Henslowe came from the Ashdown Forest, north of Lewes in Sussex, where his father had been master of the game. By the 1570s he was in London. He was a dyer who served his apprenticeship with a man called Woodward, whose widow Agnes he married. This marriage might have given him a financial leg-up and so perhaps also allowed him to purchase a patch of land in 1584 close to the Thames known as 'the Little Rose'. However, he seems already to have been a successful businessman, with properties in his native Sussex and a developing line in money-lending. By marrying Agnes Woodward he also inherited a step-daughter called Joan, who was in turn to marry the man who would contribute to the fame of the Rose, the actor Edward Alleyn.

When Henslowe arrived in London the theatrical landscape was sparse. This was a period in which theatre and its employees underwent extraordinary transformations: when Elizabeth 1 came to the throne in 1558, there were no public theatres and actors were classed with vagabonds. While Henslowe was not the first to see the possibilities of permanent public playing spaces, he was hard on the heels of James Burbage who had erected his playhouse, the Theatre, in Shoreditch in 1576, which had itself followed the Red Lion in Whitechapel built in 1567. This was a period, not of cultural *regeneration*, but of cultural *generation*.

Henslowe might be seen as a kind of Elizabethan artistic philanthropist and his other great legacy to theatre history, besides the Rose itself, was his *Diary*. This is a sort of account book of the day-to-day dealings of a theatre owner during the 1590s. As such, it has been an invaluable source of information, misinformation and scholarly debate about Elizabethan theatre practice. But Henslowe had other sides: whilst he financed the Rose, he also sought to make money from enterprises such as the ghastly spectacle of bear-baiting, considered then a perfectly respectable pastime. Henslowe was made Master of the King's Bears in 1604 – by which time the great days of the Rose had passed – and a decade after that built a duel-purpose space, inaptly named the Hope, designed to alternate between animal baiting and play-acting. Henslowe's contract for the Hope demands a 'Plaiehouse fitt & convenient in all thinges, bothe for players to playe in, and for the game of Beares and Bulls to be bayted in the same, and also a fitt and convenient Tyre house and a stage to be carryed and taken awaie ...' Ben Jonson's *Bartholomew Fair* had its premiere here as the opening play in the theatre and the actors in the Prologue make it clear why they would quickly leave the stink and noise to its other gruesome game. In the play the Scrivener, on behalf of Jonson, makes apology even to the groundlings, 'the place being as dirty as Smithfield, and as stinking every whit'.

In our own time, the architect Jon Greenfield and theatre historian Andrew Gurr have suggested that Henslowe might initially have had in mind a multi-purpose function for the Rose, although by early 1588 the local Sewer Commission was referring to it as 'the new Play-house'. The Rose has principally been associated with the plays of Christopher Marlowe and the acting of Edward Alleyn. Ben Jonson, his fellow playwright, wrote admiringly of Marlowe's 'mighty line' and Alleyn is forever associated with a role Marlowe wrote for him – Tamburlaine in the two parts of *Tamburlaine the Great*, which was one of the most popular plays of the time. Alleyn became synonymous with:

> ... the Scythian Tamburlaine
> Threat'ning the world with high astounding terms
> And scourging kingdoms with his conquering sword.

By default, the Southbank Rose over time became wrongly known as the place of noisy rhetoric, in comparison with the more sophisticated Curtain, Theatre and Globe of Burbage and Shakespeare. Andrew Gurr, by chance closely associated with the modern development of Shakespeare's Globe, has said somewhat scathingly, 'It was "majestic" parts that Alleyn excelled in and there is reason to believe that Alleyn's violence of voice and gesture in his most famous parts established a tradition of exaggeration ...' It's rather unfair on Alleyn, on the Rose and, for that matter, on Marlowe too. The Rose repertoire must have been extensive, although we are not able to give a very detailed assessment: of the 280 plays which Henslowe mentions in his *Diary* only 29 seem to have survived, and so it is simplistic to ascribe such a 'house-style' to the Rose. What we do know is that it was not 'Shakespeare's Rose', which it is so often misrepresented as in modern times, not least by our own contemporary Rose publicity. *Titus Andronicus* and possibly *Henry V1 Part 1* were given their first performances at the Rose and it is not inconceivable that Shakespeare acted on the Rose stage. However, the playwright who most deserves to be associated with the Rose is Christopher Marlowe.

Henslowe's invaluable *Diary* survived because, on his death in 1616 – an event in theatre history inevitably overshadowed by the demise of Shakespeare in the same year – he left it to his son-in-law, Edward 'Ned' Alleyn. Alleyn, who had retired as an actor a decade and a half before, as the Rose itself had fallen into disuse, had by then added wealth to his distinction as a player. He was soon to found Dulwich College –

'the College of God's gift' – with the purpose of educating twelve 'poor scholars' on a part of his large estates in what is now London SE. All Alleyn's papers, which included the *Diary*, were left to the College on his death in 1626 where they can still be seen, especially by the 1500 school students of Dulwich today, who are now somewhat richer than their original predecessors.

Since John Payne Collier's 1845 version of Henslowe's *Diary* (albeit with added forgeries) Henslowe has provided scholars hungry for any tit-bit of detail or document on 'Shakespeare's Theatre' with food for discussion and elaboration. This has not precluded fascination with the question of who Henslowe was. Was the man who built one of the earliest purpose-built theatres in England a lover of theatre particularly, or a man with an eye for a business opportunity? Economic and cultural development have always gone hand in hand. As Peter Thomson wrote, Henslowe was 'the shrewdest of all theatrical speculators'. That is not to say that he was the illiterate and money-driven speculator characterised by Victorian historians and most who followed them. This particular notion has been effectively challenged and debunked by Carol Chillington Rutter in her *Documents of the Rose Playhouse*. Professor Rutter, it just so happens, was once married to the actor Barrie Rutter, who would himself be the first professional actor to play in public on Kingston's re-born Rose stage.

It was not until 1989 that it became evident that Henslowe's legacy to theatre was unimaginably greater – simply by virtue of the discovery of the physical foundations of his building. It was well known that in 1586/7 he had built and opened the Rose Theatre on his newly acquired land, just as we knew that competition at the turn of the century had killed it off. By 1603 – the year of the death of Queen Elizabeth 1 – the Rose too disappeared from view, only to re-emerge from the Thameside mud through the delicate trowel work of the Museum of London archaeologists three hundred and eighty five years later. Carol Rutter captured the significance: 'As, stone by stone, Henslowe's playhouse emerged from oblivion, the archaeology was able to give material shape to the contracts, the accounts, the miscellaneous references to the Rose scattered across Henslowe's *Diary*: documents seemed re-produced in three dimensions'.

The significance of all this in 1989 for the campaign for a theatre in Kingston as yet remained obscure.

The discovery of that archaeology caused a storm, affecting the cultural and political life of the nation: the land was now a piece of real estate and the developers had planning permission for a vast office block. Planning had already been passed for a new multi-storey building, south of Southwark Bridge. When the discovery was announced in the press that the foundations of an Elizabethan theatre lay beneath, the site became occupied by a host of people in the best traditions of English radicalism, including many of the leaders of the theatrical profession, determined to prevent damage to a heritage find. Peggy Ashcroft, then in her last years, defied the bulldozers and held a candlelit vigil, alongside other theatrical and cultural luminaries. No other drama ever boasted such a cast list: Janet Suzman, Judi Dench, Ralph Fiennes, Dustin Hoffman, Ian McKellen and many more. Speeches were made both on the site and soon in Parliament, where the Secretary of State for the Environment, Nicholas Ridley, came under furious attack for failing to list the site as a national monument. The ailing Laurence Olivier gave out what was to be his last public statement, read to the protesters at the site, saying the discovery was 'a vitally important part of our theatrical history'. Olivier died little more than a month later. Peter Hall, who at the time had no idea that he would become the first director of the re-born Rose of Kingston, said that to allow the bulldozers in to continue the office block development was a vandalism tantamount to 'demolishing the Parthenon to build a car park'.

The excitement at the discovery of Henslowe's theatre was accompanied by some surprises. The perception of the character of most Elizabethan outdoor theatres, or amphitheatres – the Theatre, the Globe, the Rose, the Swan – was that they were large, indicated by extant documents. Three features of the unique archaeology of the Rose stood out, significant because they would each have affected *how* a player played and *what* an audience experienced; they were also to have a telling affect on how we approached building the theatre in Kingston a decade later. The three surprises were the polygonal shape of the theatre, the shape of the stage, and the surprisingly small size of the whole amphitheatre space. It was said that when Ian McKellen went down to the archaeological dig his first response was, 'Well, you don't have to shout in here', so struck was he by the intimacy of the space. Many years later – in 2014 – I was challenged by an editor to reference McKellen's remark for an academic paper. I ransacked my notes and papers, but could not find it. By the most curious of coincidences I was sitting with my daughter in the Rose a very few days later watching a performance of Brian Friel's *Translations*. McKellen was sitting in the seat immediately behind so I was able to ask him if he had said that. 'Do you know', he said, enthusiastically, 'I can't remember if I did say that, but if I didn't I certainly should have done, so I'm saying it now!' And so it is referenced as a footnote in *Actors' Conversations at the Rose Theatres* (Cahiers Élisabéthains, Volume 88, MUP, Autumn 2015) as 'Affirmed in personal communication, 23 April 2014'. This would all provide food for thought in building a modern version of the Rose, but it has also caused some of us to rethink the impact that the original theatre must have had.

The building of the proposed and contentious office block was delayed in 1989, but not halted: a new design was developed and the resulting structure, Rose Court, is now on stilts to allow access to the foundations of the Elizabethan Rose – the Rose Playhouse, Southwark – beneath. It was not for several years that this exciting archaeological discovery became linked to Kingston's theatrical ambitions, following the failure of the National Lottery application of 1997.

Kingston's Rose is, of course a modern building and not an open-air amphitheatre. It has two 'galleries' and the raised stalls area, and now the front stalls. For many years after opening, the cheapest seats were sitting on the floor and before that the floor was very much lower and used as standing space during the Season in the Shell, just as the 'groundlings' in the 1590s stood. It remains uncertain whether the original Rose had two or three galleries. Unlike its sister, Shakespeare's Globe, our Rose is not an attempt at historical representation. But the design of the main auditorium is effectively in its ground dimensions a reflection of her forebear. The architect used the archaeology as a blueprint for the main auditorium, and so the geometric relationships between actor and audience are very similar to those which must have existed for Edward Alleyn and his audiences four hundred years ago.

·

The nature and quality of the actor-audience communication at the original Rose were evidently very different to anything which had previously been supposed by theatre historians. Kingston's Rose does not pretend to be an accurate replica: it is a modern theatre, which attempts to ensure that the spatial relationship between the stage and auditorium resembles as closely as possible the original. In our opening season 'in the shell' we had our pit, with standing, but that has since given way to modern demands for more comfort. The 1587 Rose was a fourteen-sided, not entirely regular polygon; Kingston's Rose has eleven large sides, with ten smaller sections, an arrangement which enables best use of the footprint available to the development, whilst preserving as closely as possible a relationship with the original. The *measurements*, however, are telling: the external diameter of the *original* was 72 feet, and in the new theatre 73 feet 7 inches; the inner 'yard' of the Alleyn's Rose was 49 feet and of its offspring 49 feet 6 inches. So they are very similar.

The other important feature which emerged from the archaeology was the shape of the stage: the excavations revealed the original dimensions of the stage. Whilst there have inevitably been changes and adaptations as productions demanded, we began with an upstage width of approximately 37 feet tapering to 27 feet downstage, and only 16 feet 6 inches deep. This is the 'lozenge' shape and is very similar – to a matter of inches – to the original. Previous assumptions had been that Elizabethan stages were 'thrusts', platforms projecting out into the audience. These assumptions were based on two primary sources: the first was a document known as De Witt's drawing of the Swan Theatre, which was built quite close to the original Rose in 1595, and the second an order to the carpenter Peter Street – who also built the Globe – for Henslowe's new Fortune Theatre, which was built in 1600 and which had largely replaced the smaller Rose within a few years. Each had a thrust stage, but the Rose did not.

The exciting 1989 archaeological activity was happening on London's Southbank only shortly after the formation of KTT, but it would take several years for it to have a particular influence. So in this respect delay was a distinct advantage to the Kingston project.

The 1587 Rose: a reconstructive cutaway view of the first Rose by William Dudley, incorporating material by John Greenfield and C. Walter Hodges.

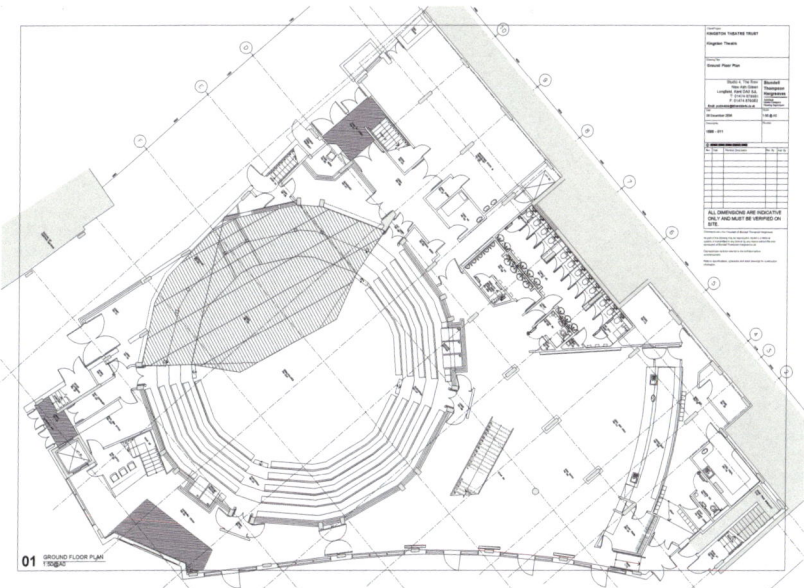

Ground floor plan Rose Theatre Kingston

Auditorium under construction

Season in the Shell: 'Groundlings' standing in the Pit

Lighting Gantry under construction

'Groundlings' seated in the Pit   *Photo Rachael Lowndes*

Theatre exterior during The Season in The Raw 2004

New stalls seating. Pit done January 2019; rear stalls summer 2023. Works
funded by Backstage Trust   *Photo Rachael Lowndes*

Robin Hutchinson

Frank Whately

David Jacobs

Geoff Howard

Diana Robertson, Roger Chown, Katie Randerson - Founder Friends and
Committee Members, Kingston Theatre Friends.

Gerry Gunn   David Fletcher

Photo Surrey Comet

Peter Hall and Mary Reid

Stephen Unwin

Christopher Haydon

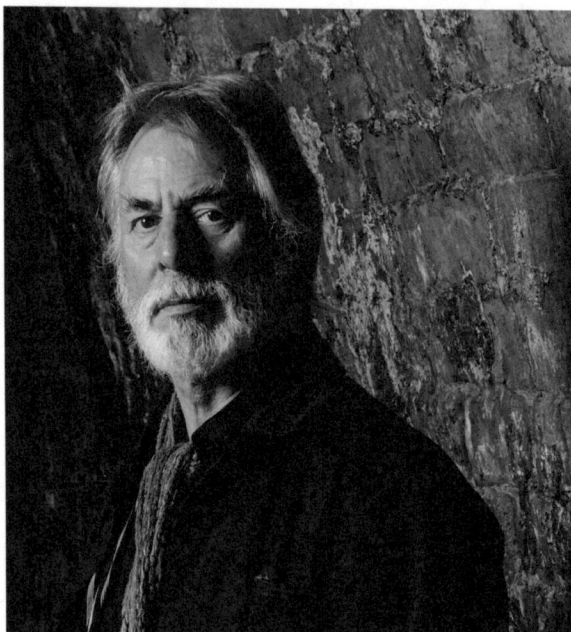

Barrie Rutter who
directed Northern
Broadsides' production
of Henry V and played
Chorus in the Season
in The Shell 2003

Don Juan in Kingston, the community play conceived and directed by Phil
Willmott 2003

Judi Dench and Friends 2004
Left to Right: <u>Back</u> Colin Salmon, Samantha Bond, Peter Hall, Judi Dench, Charles
Dance, David Jacobs, Rebecca Hall, Martin Jarvis, Alan Dobie, Julian Glover.
<u>Foreground</u> David Oyelowo, Samuel West, Dan Stevens, Michael Pennington, Tim
Pigott-Smith   *Photo Nobby Clark*

Judi Dench and Friends 2004
Chicken Shed Theatre   *Photo Nobby Clark*

As You Like It
Season in The Raw 2004

Rebecca Hall as Rosalind and
David Stevens as Orlando
Photo Nobby Clark

Phillip Voss as Jaques

Photo Nobby Clark

Nicholas Le Provost as Vanya and Neil Pearson as Astrov in *Chekhov's Uncle Vanya* 2008

Photo – Wiltshire Times

Judi Dench as Titania and Oliver Chris as Bottom
A Midsummer Night's Dream 2010

Photo - Tristram Kenton

Phoebe Thomas as Hetty Feather
Hetty Feather 2014   Photo Helen Maybanks

Peter Brook and Peter Hall at the Rose's third birthday in 2011   Photo Paul Milsom

11
The First Theatre of the Twenty First Century

With the Millennium approaching, we wanted to take advantage of this watershed moment. We had begun to refer to the theatre as 'The First Theatre of the Twenty First Century' and very much hoped that it would be! Colin Bloxham did some groundwork on developing plans for a Millennium Festival which would in some way feature the historic town centre of Kingston. Tony Anstee chaired a group of KTT members, comprising David Nield, Robin Hutchinson, Colin Bloxham and me, to oversee the process. We quickly adopted the title of 'The Claiming the Space Festival' – the 'Space' being both the land the theatre would be built on *and* its shell. This would make its contribution to raising the public's awareness, whilst at the same time ensuring that there would be no turning back.

It was at this point that two people who were to work selflessly for the theatre over the ensuing years joined us. Mary Reid had recently become an RBK nominee to the Board, effectively in place of her husband, Ian. For all that she had had some considerable sympathy with the arts centre idea, Mary threw herself wholeheartedly into the work of the Trust and was particularly concerned that the Millennium opportunity did not slip. Ironically, Lottery funds were available for Millennium celebrations around the country and our application on this occasion was successful, and £25k was forthcoming. As this was the first monies to come to the Trust, Alan Stephenson joined as treasurer and began an association which has gone well beyond merely tending the purse strings. Both Mary and Alan remain great ambassadors.

As the artistic director of 'Claiming the Space', I devised an episodic pageant which would comprise a series of light-hearted and entertaining scenes drawn from Kingston's real or imagined past. The idea was to involve as many people as possible and, having determined a scenic structure, different groups both already existing or brought together for the event would develop their chosen scene. Each would represent a particular Guild – Vintners, Wool Merchants, Carpenters and so on – to give a further sense of Kingston's trading past and mediaeval associations. While there was the odd gesture in the direction of historical accuracy, it was a celebration of imagination and the idea of performance. Large numbers came to an open meeting in late September 1999, and the proposals seemed to tickle most fancies. The Guilds went to work.

We played three performances in May 2000. As with mediaeval pageant plays, each scene took place at particular 'stations' beginning outside the new Bentall's Centre where the audience for each performance would gather. The narrative thread was an interplay between a Mrs and Mr Kingston, two characters played by my daughter Martha and me, and we led the spectators from one scene to the next. So at All Saints' Church they saw the Parish Church Choir perform the Coronation of King Athelstan with wry references to further crownings. Tiffin School in the guise of the Brewers' Guild, in celebration of John and Thomas Tiffin the seventeenth century brewing brothers who founded the school, created the Crowning of Eadwig the Debaucher. The audience then left the precincts of the Church to be conducted, along with improvised banter by Mrs and Mr Kingston, to the Memorial Gardens where the Royal Charter was given by King John in a scene, stretching fact into fable, which also featured an appearance by Robin Hood and his merry men and women. In the Apple Market Julius Caesar, who might have crossed the Thames at Kingston, time travelled down several centuries to meet Sir Thomas Wyatt and Queen Mary. The Elizabethan age was celebrated in the Market Place by the Spring Grove Players in the guise of Wool Merchants. Finally, on the site where the theatre would be built the Green Theatre of New Malden offered a view of the town emerging from the Victorian age as

'Inventive Kingston' in a satirically played mask sequence. And then the whole company of pageant players joined them for a finale, written by the pageant's musical director David Nield. More than two thousand followed the three performances, which had involved enough participants to pack St. John's School playground on our one full group rehearsal. The space for the theatre was claimed and few people now doubted the theatre would be built: where the rude mechanicals had stepped, Titania and Oberon would play – as, indeed, a decade later they did in Peter Hall's production with Dame Judi Dench as the Fairy Queen and Charles Edwards as her jealous fairy spouse in *A Midsummer Night's Dream*.

It is interesting that attempts to get Kingston University to take on one of the pageant scenes failed. Within a few months, however, I left Tiffin School after nearly three decades to create a drama degree course at Kingston University and later a School of Performance. Drama became, in the words of the Vice Chancellor Sir Peter Scott, 'a flagship of the University'. A decade later, the University had become a mainstay, in performance terms, of the International Youth Arts Festival, as well as one of the two principal partners in the Rose Theatre itself.

It was envisaged that amongst other influences, the pageant would be valuable in helping to develop a Friends' organisation. Geoff Howard was anxious that the timing of this be controlled to maximise both its impact and its contribution to the fundraising appeal and it would be another year before the Friends' foundation. But one of the Spring Grove Players stood ready and waiting and would later spearhead the Friends.

Almost inevitably, costs were mounting and there was still no solution to RBK's withdrawal from their 1989 commitment to fund a large part of the capital fit-out costs and give some annual revenue funding. It was now calculated that the project would cost a total of around £8 million. Of this, approximately £4 million was already in place in the form of the site, the proposed shell and input already made in terms of development costs. So we needed to identify a further £4 million, a marked rise from the original appeal figure which had been estimated at £1 million eleven years earlier.

Howard listed three other potential sources. The first was an additional capital contribution from St. George, which might be the £850,000 derived from the sale of the fly tower 'air above the theatre' (provided that St George did not succeed in arguing that the changes we had recently made would not increase the cost to them of the shell). Next was the securing of one or two major contributions which might become linked with the naming of the theatre. The third was the development of partnership arrangements for future use of the theatre, which might themselves open further opportunities. Beyond this, approaches began to be made to grant-making trusts and foundations which support arts initiatives.

It had become a matter of urgency in the months leading up to the Millennium that Geoff Howard should be released from the role of administrator to the Trust which he had taken on to see us through the 'dark' years. Equally, the appeal campaign would also need to have admin-istration on the ground, to assist Howard. Of course, a new appointment should have been made by the Trust, but as ever there were no funds. Some months earlier, St George had given £20,000 to the project and as a first step this money was put towards the appointment and the establishment of some sort of office space. Small beer, but it was a start and Charlotte Gill was appointed Campaign Administrator late in 1999.

So the year 2000 had begun auspiciously. Michael Holden worked with great energy to develop the new plans for the theatre, whilst at the same time difficult negotiations continued with St. George over the nature of the shell and their contribution to it. We were most keen to avoid the need to go to arbitration as this would delay things at a time when, thanks to Holden, there was a good momentum. Planning permission for the amended design was granted by the middle of 2000, which included the provision of the flats in place of the fly-tower. It was estimated then that, following the provision of the shell, the fitting out of the theatre would cost £4.2 million.

The central feature of the new design was the main auditorium, which was based on the archaeological discovery of Henslowe's Rose Theatre of 1587. The capacity was estimated at 1100, based on the idea of spectators standing in the pit and with seating on three levels. This one detail gave an imaginative impetus to the project: as the appeal literature was developed Shakespeare's support was enlisted:

Think when we talk of horses, that you see them,
Printing their proud hooves in the receiving earth:
For it is your thoughts that now must deck our kings.

Prologue, *Henry V*

There would also be a studio theatre with a capacity of 220, and a rehearsal room which would double as a smaller performance space with at most 90 seats. In the event this last space, although provided in the finished shell, was never realised in the fit-out as it was needed as technical space. There was in this plan the art gallery, foyers, bars and a café which largely survived through the next stages of development. One feature and a particular aspiration of Michael Holden was a double helix staircase, but sadly it was never built as we had to accept a cheaper option: the current central stairs. Whatever we might want to put in or take out in terms of developing design elements, we could not change the basic boot-shaped footprint available.

Artistic plans were beginning to show greater ambition. Since the removal of a former commitment to some revenue funding by RBK, the question about initiating repertory work had been shelved for the time being. However, we developed plans for professional 'festival seasons' which might feature actors who had a contact with the theatre: Janet Suzman, Imelda Staunton, David Yelland, Kevin Whately and Jonny Lee Miller were names brought into conversations – largely because they had some sort of association and supported what we were doing. The nature of the new design encouraged aspirations to bring the work of the Royal Exchange Theatre, Manchester, West Yorkshire Playhouse and the RSC's Swann productions to Kingston. Braham Murray at Manchester and Jude Kelly, still artistic director in Leeds, were encouraging. Adrian Noble was more guarded: when he saw drawings, he thought the theatre would be successful for audiences, but his concern was that, with the RSC still based in the Barbican and rehearsing in Clapham, a third leg in Kingston would be difficult for actors needing to travel. I sent Noble a train timetable with details of Waterloo/ Clapham Junction to Surbiton trains, with six or seven an hour and the quickest at fifteen minutes each way, but received no further reply. Another commitment was to a major festival of youth theatre every summer which has, subsequently, borne fruit: the International Youth Arts Festival ran successfully from the opening year, until its recent transformation into Fuse International. In a prescient note, our appeal brochure added, 'the theatre's future association with Kingston University will be invaluable'.

To bind all the parties – RBK, the Kingston Theatre Trust and St. George – into this new plan, we devised a signing ceremony on the theatre site, where the developer had established a billboard advertising the whole development. Bruce Macdonald had recently been appointed Chief Executive at the Guildhall, beginning a distinguished period in that role. He signed on behalf of the Royal Borough. Ian Dobie signed on behalf of St. George. I invited my old student and friend Jonny Lee Miller to sign for KTT. Jonny was born and grew up in Kingston and his stage career as an actor had really begun, at the age of thirteen, as a lead in *The Ragged Child* in the year in which the Arts Working Party had first convened – 1986. He played Joe Cooper, a street orphan in Victorian London, and the role had taken him from the Tiffin School stage, to the Bergen Festival in Norway, to Edinburgh's International Festival, to Sadler's Wells and finally onto BBC TV. He was now becoming one of a brave new generation of actors, most memorably in Danny Boyle's *Trainspotting* It would be two more decades before he played the former Prime Minister John Major in *The Crown*. It seemed right that the Trust should be represented by a youthful figure, with local connections.

The Board itself needed an injection of new blood. Brian Willman, who many years before had been a leading light in the second Arts for Kingston campaign and had been a member of the 1986 Working Party, joined the Trust in late 1999. Half way through the first year of the new millennium Gail Cunningham, Richard House, Emma de Souza and David Errington broadened the Trust's expertise. Gail Cunningham would bring the University right into the centre of the theatre's affairs at this critical development stage. She was Dean of the University's largest faculty, a Pro Vice-Chancellor and an articulate and committed theatre-goer. Richard House was to play an invaluable role as the technical elements of the theatre were created, but also brought a strong corporate legal mind to the Trust. He combined being head of the legal department at the Mitsubishi Bank with his roles as a trustee of the Pleasance Theatre and as an effective professional stage lighting designer, not least on many of my productions. David Errington was an established financial expert with a global company and a local theatre enthusiast. Emma de Souza, who had played a leading role in my National Youth Music Theatre production of *October's Children* a decade before, was already developing her career at the Society of London Theatres, in which she is now a leading light.

Following Peter Winfield's death, David Jacobs had, with typical selflessness, stepped into his shoes to lead the appeal for the theatre fit out. In order to raise the profile again in preparation for the public launch in a few months time, David hosted a reception at the Garrick Club, at which Gail Cunningham, Michael Holden and I gave presentations. Sir Peter Hall, who had recently become the Chancellor of Kingston University, was one of those who had agreed to be a Vice President and he was joined by a large group – as these things need to be – of the well-known and the well-oiled. It certainly gave the theatre a national rather than local flavour, with Jerry Hall, Brian Rix, Elspet Gray, Kevin Whately, Richard Briers, Janet Suzman and Ronnie Corbett amongst some of the better known faces. We even enlisted the England cricket captain, Alec Stewart, whom I had nominally coached as an Under 12 cricketer at Tiffin School. Of course, his cricketing refinement was largely the result of parental guidance in the shape of his father Mickey, by now the England coach, but Alec agreed to have his name attached as long as he did not have to *say* anything about theatre. Many did more than merely lend their names: Jerry Hall, for instance, gave valuable help in a number of ways over the years, including donating a Pete Townshend guitar towards fundraising and becoming President of the Rose Friends, until she was whisked away by an Australian newspaper magnate.

Much of the work was now overseen by a Theatre Management Committee, chaired by Gail Cunningham and including Robin Hutchinson, Richard House and me. David Errington and Alan Stephenson, our two financial experts on the Trust, were also involved and did some of the vital work negotiating a loan from RBK, in the first instance of £900,000. They worked with Tony Knights, RBK's Director of Finance. Knights was one of those people involved in major local projects who, as a civil servant, receive scant recognition. He worked quietly behind the scenes for many years to help us keep the theatre project going and when times became difficult he would engage his ingenuity to find solutions. If the odd local authority mandarin, in our experience, could puff himself up like a popinjay, Tony was the antithesis of this and more than once he contributed to help shield us against stumbling.

Building was soon to begin and Michael Holden offered himself as the Project Manager. He had played as Jack of All Trades previously, and we welcomed his sheer energy and confident all-round commitment. The construction of the shell began in March 2001. It was a thrilling moment: Robin and I stood on the pavement nearby and physically pinched each other to check we were not deluded that at last we were underway – more than twenty years after we began our campaign. As the bulldozers began to line up, I had asked Imelda Staunton to come down to Kingston to cut the first clod. Meanwhile, unbeknownst to me, Michael Holden extended the same invitation to Felicity Kendal! And so it was that each had donned a hard hat and a pair of wellies, shared a shovel and kick-started the building together, fifteen years after the Arts Working Party had formally proposed that Kingston should build a theatre.

Later in the summer, on the evening of the Summer Solstice, 21st June 2001 Peter Hall, who had been appointed Chancellor of Kingston University the previous year, now as a Vice President of the Rose Appeal officially launched the public fundraising campaign to build 'the First Theatre of the 21st Century'. He enjoyed telling the story of how, when David Jacobs had a year earlier, sent him the theatre plans and invited him to become involved he had groaned: 'Oh no, not *another* theatre!' But he then looked at the designs and was thrilled: it was, 'the theatre I had dreamed of all my life'. He neatly captured the essence of what we were trying to do when he described ours as, 'a new theatre taking inspiration from theatre history and then loosing all shackles with the past, with an innovative design and artistic ambition that fully recognises the key role of young people in artistic creativity'. His comment also had a sub-text: there was a potential now which needed to be much more fully developed in terms of artistic possibility. I thought then that we would talk to him further for advice, but had no inkling of what it would lead to. That evening the National Youth Music Theatre gave a preview in the Market Place of what would become a hit show, *The Dreaming*, by Howard Goodall and Charles Hart. At the time it was hoped that the NYMT would become a major partner in the enterprise, but this was now the twilight of the NYMT's phenomenal years. The company which had been described by Peter Whitebrook in *The Scotsman* as 'Britain's greatest youth company' and by Andrew Lloyd Webber as 'the best youth music theatre in the world' was about to enter a decade of financial struggle. However, two of the leading players in *The Dreaming*, Ben Barnes and Sarah Brown, became two of the first Kingston University undergraduate drama students on my new drama course the following Autumn. Ben would go on to be the Drama Department's first First Class Honours graduate, prior to a career which was immediately successful on stage and in film. He played in *The History Boys* for the National Theatre, as the lead of Trevor Nunn's stage version of *Birdsong*, as the title character in the film *A Picture of Dorian Gray* and as Prince Caspian in Disney's *The Chronicles of Narnia*.

Charlie Gill left the project in Autumn 2001, to return to the National Theatre, and her place was taken by Louise Coles, which turned out to be a brilliant appointment. Records had been maintained over the years of people with an interest in a Friends' organisation and this had been boosted by the Pageant in the previous year. An open meeting was held at the University on the morning of Saturday 10th November 2001 inviting all those with an interest in forming a Friends' group to support the provision of the proposed theatre. Michael Holden enthusiastically presented the plans as work in progress and Geoff Howard and Louise Coles led discussion of fundraising plans and needs. Brian Willman represented the Trustees. From this meeting emerged the Friends under the chairmanship of Roger Chown, another of those 'Kingstonians' Peter Hall referred to with such admiration. The Friends, led by Roger, would make such a vital contribution to the new theatre.

The Friends membership grew rapidly in numbers, enthusiasm and action. Chown's contribution in first motivating them and later taking on a role in the theatre's corporate development has had a significant impact and he became a central figure at the Rose. In the first instance, he led the Friends as they raised the public's awareness of the theatre in a variety of ways; at last, it was now no longer left to individual members of the Trust to beat the drum. Chown became a director of the Trust and, owing to the success of his recruitment of members, he was able to represent a diversity of opinions and ideas from within the community.

The work of the Friends was focused on raising awareness and building an audience, which they succeeded in sustaining despite further delays in the future before the final opening. When that time did arrive, there was a ready band of volunteers who would be and still are crucial to the running of the theatre. An appeal also went out to the local community seeking Founder Friends to join the ranks of the rapidly growing Friends' organisation by making gifts that would be recognised by the ubiquitous 'named seats' – an apparently obligatory component of all theatre fundraising initiatives.

The workload was increasing, but the means to fund it was not. Louise Coles was not only administering the appeal and also the KTT, but now we planned a season of work in the completed shell of the theatre, including a community play. The Friends' was functioning smoothly, which took some pressure away. In addition, Nigel Duffin, an original Friend and pageant player in the opening Athelstan scene, was now giving time in the office. Katie Randerson was leading on Publicity and efficiently harnessing the Friends. Elinor Burdall had recently been recruited to administer the increasing number of Trust meetings and she quickly established herself in her quiet and distinctive way: she was able to see the absurd in the most earnestly drab situations, which her face reflected with exquisite timing, like a series of frames in a silent movie, even as she was recording minutes in precise detail at high speed. At the same time, Michael Holden was working beyond his brief, as were so many others, taking on tasks to maintain momentum.

Amidst the energy, enthusiasm, selfless commitment and ingenuity one element remained disappointingly inert: the appeal did not succeed in attracting the one or two really big donors which we had hoped for to replace the withdrawal of the Borough's original capital commitment. With the shell nearing completion we desperately wanted to continue the work on into the fit-up and the opening of the theatre.

12
Play Making

Two weeks after the Summer Solstice launch, the shell of the building was nearing completion and I suggested to David Jacobs that I should bring together a group to review the artistic policy. This theatre had the potential to be very much more than a receiving house.

The group would comprise the original artistic committee – Robin Hutchinson, Colin Bloxham (to keep RBK actively involved, but also because he was always a well of good ideas) and me. We would enhance the group with others: I was particularly keen to have younger people involved. We would consult with a variety of individuals and organisations. There were several reasons why this was overdue, but the most pressing was that increasingly the pace was being forced by Michael Holden, with assumptions made, rather than proposals fully discussed. As a consultant appointed to develop a business plan, but now also working on the development of the shell, Holden had been assiduous as a servant of the Trust. He brought his wide-ranging experience of a variety of the technical aspects of theatre and theatre building to bear, he worked tirelessly developing plans, often delivering documents to individual trust members at all hours of the day and night. He was always available for discussion – and this in the context of delays and doubts and uncertainties. However, some details became documented without discussion.

Holden had begun developing a more detailed business plan, which assumed the theatre would be run, principally, as a receiving house with a Chief Executive. We had always argued that the theatre would be able to receive high class product, for example the Royal Shakespeare Company's Swan productions, those from the West Yorkshire Playhouse and from

117

Manchester Royal Exchange. However, Holden's original developments of the Studio had assumed, somewhat bizarrely, that the Orange
Tree Theatre in Richmond would transfer some of its more successful
productions down the road to Kingston. Some thought this odd, not least
Sam Walters the Orange Tree's founder and artistic director, with whom
I had many discussions. Sam was later made an Honorary Doctor of the
University and enthusiastically offered workshops in the Rose Studio
to my postgraduate drama students, but he never thought Orange Tree
transfers would have any point.

Holden's first *Business Plan & Project Study* had appeared in October
1999. He had been quite right to assert that we needed a theatre design
before producing an effective business plan. Now that we had settled on
a theatre influenced by the original Rose I could not think that such a
theatre should only receive work from other theatres. Michael agreed, I felt
somewhat reluctantly, that there might be certain productions created in
the theatre, but these would be strictly isolated, almost quarantined, from
the other work from a financial point of view: they would be in limited
'festival' seasons, he suggested. This was not of itself an unwise proposal,
but it did rather detract from an aspiration that the theatre should make
waves beyond our small stretch of the Thames. By early 2002, with 60%
of the shell completed, Holden gave us a second draft of his business plan.
In the Introduction he noted we were building 'a unique theatre' and so
one which would not 'compete for product with existing theatres [in the
catchment area]'. He stressed that it would be 'capable of sustaining itself ...
provided that production activity is limited ... ' He noted that the theatre
must accomplish much for Kingston, including raising its reputation
'regionally, nationally and internationally'. Throughout, he returned to the
theme: the theatre must, 'present productions largely generated by other
theatres and producers'. There seemed to me to be some inherent contradictions here.

There was another difficulty, which began to emerge. Holden had for
a while during its very early days become the Chief Executive of Shakespeare's Globe on the Southbank, having formerly acted as one of the
consultants on that project. The idea of building a theatre based on the
1587 Rose might just prove fortuitous: it became evident that he was

beginning to anticipate a similar role in Kingston, with *his* vision of how the theatre should operate prevailing. He had said when interviewed for the job of writing a business plan that one of the benefits of taking on Michael Holden Associates was that he would remain afterwards to see plans into action. I had not at the time seen the significance of this. Now, in a section on the executive, he returned again to his familiar theme: 'the chief executive post will reflect the emphasis of the Kingston Theatre on receiving other theatres' product ...' Was the Trust being backed into a corner?

The political backing had come primarily for the sound reason (a reason which has not changed) that the economic, social and cultural benefits to the town were potentially considerable. The theatre must make a significant contribution to Kingston's development, particularly to the economy and ambiance of the town at night. While the demand that the theatre be able to 'wash its face' – this metaphor for financial security – was a part of the initial aims which Michael Holden Associates were charged with, investment now would have great economic benefits in the mid- to long-term for the town. It needed a braver vision.

True to its word another player now became increasingly influential. Kingston University was expanding quickly and its pro-active engagement was significant. For me events had inevitably taken an interesting turn as I was now leading the creation of a Drama Honours Degree course at the University. Kingston University would evidently benefit directly from the theatre and so, provided the theatre was distinctive enough, there would also be another source of funding. For the theatre merely to be a receiving house, distinction would be lacking.

During the artistic policy review, we went out to canvas a range of opinion. Emma de Souza had been a director of KTT, but had left lest her Society of London Theatres work should be compromised; however, she offered valuable thoughts. (A decade later Emma rejoined the Trust). Richard House contributed from his wide range of experience. Hannah Yelland was then a young actress who had grown up in the area, her father the distinguished classical actor David Yelland; ten years later Hannah would be nominated for a Tony Award for *Brief Encounter* on Broadway. Josie Rourke was just beginning her career, but offered strong and attractive opinions – which will not be a surprise in the light of her subsequent distinction as a director. None was 'a name' at that point, but each brought a fresh mind, unconstrained by position and attitudes formed over years. Each is now distinguished in their field. We had talks, too, with experienced people: John Elsom offered a clear idea of how he thought the theatre should progress which, he argued, meant using effective theatre consultancy. Jude Kelly, then artistic director of West Yorkshire Playhouse, offered invaluable advice and support which continued over years. Sue Storr, at that time the director of the Conservatoire for Dance and Drama, offered positive thoughts. Michael Holden had, of course, a strong sense of what he envisaged. Towards the end of our deliberations I had two meetings with Sir Peter Hall, which were to prove defining.

I wrote a report to the Trust in June 2002 and outlined three potential ways forward. The first was that we could accept the programming as outlined in the current Business Plan, leading to the appointment of a Chief Executive. This would mean that the theatre should principally be a receiving house of work created by other producing houses. There would be a 'Festival Season' of productions promoted by the theatre. A second potential route was to engage a separate theatre consultancy group to explore the feasibility of various approaches to programming, as a preliminary to appointing a Chief Executive/ Artistic Director. These might challenge the assumptions made in the current Business Plan and suggest a variety of approaches to the management of the theatre and the creation of the programme. The third approach would be to appoint an Artistic Director and ensure that her/his vision would be engaged in the development of the creative policy, the refinement of the Business Plan and would contribute to the internal design. This might also give an added impetus to the fundraising process.

The first approach was explicit in the latest business plan and so it was effectively championed by Michael Holden. Its principal tenet was that the theatre would be a receiving house and therefore controlled by a chief executive, rather than an artistic director. Whilst we ultimately diverged from the central thrust of Holden's report, there were good ideas, some of which survive to this day: youth theatre seasons 'of national importance' are reflected now in the former International Youth Arts Festival, now

Fuse International; a Christmas production which establishes 'a tradition of presenting an appropriate musical production which has individual appeal' has been brilliantly realised since 2014, initially over several years by Ciaran McGonville's work. Holden also proposed a season of classical theatre, especially from the Elizabethan and Jacobean period, to reflect the theatre's roots. For a number of years, following Stephen Unwin's artistic directorship, Robert O'Dowd, as Chief Executive, with Jerry Gunn, as Executive Producer, oversaw the creation of Rose Theatre productions, both independently and in collaboration, using a number of directors. However, even then, production played a more central role than Michael Holden envisaged.

The idea of rule by consultancy in the first instance – largely proposed and represented by John Elsom – effectively challenged the assumptions made in the business plan. This seemed to be winding back the clock, suggesting that a consultancy could do the work which the Artistic Review Group had already undertaken (perhaps with a different outcome) and with yet more money spent on consultancy fees.

Far more persuasive – and, indeed, stimulating and exciting – were the arguments of those who saw the extraordinary potential of the theatre we were building. Jude Kelly was unequivocal: it was an exceptional and challenging space which would stimulate new work and it should, at least in part, be a producing house. Josie Rourke, with the clarity of thinking for which she is now well known, came to Kingston one evening to say it must not be consigned as a receiving house. The majority of others consulted agreed and these views were endorsed overwhelmingly by the Trust and I was asked to explore how this might be best effected.

Jude Kelly came to Kingston early one summer morning and I took her onto the site where good progress was being made building the shell. Jude had recently announced that she was leaving West Yorkshire Playhouse, where she had worked with such distinction as its first artistic director. When Trevor Nunn stepped down as Artistic Director of the RNT it was generally assumed that two people headed the field to succeed him: Jude herself and the 'house insider' and betting favourite Nick Hytner. The latter was duly appointed, but Jude had already developed other aspirations: when I asked her if she would be interested in taking on Kingston's new theatre, she said that she had a number of projects in mind and she was probably relishing her relative freedom to take on a variety of challenges. She was already establishing her Metal Culture spaces to enable artistic explorations. Her renowned production for English National Opera of *On The Town* was waiting around the corner. Much later, she would become for twelve years Artistic Director of the Southbank Centre, and its extraordinary success between 2006 and 2016 is a tribute to her ingenuity. She went on to create the Women of the World Foundation to which she now directs all her energies. She remained a creative support to changes in Kingston over a number of years: she was someone I had frequent recourse to for advice, help and active involvement: she has not only an impressive knowledge and understanding of the arts and arts organisations, but also a willingness and generosity in sharing and helping. She became my first Visiting Professor of Drama at Kingston University.

A week or so after Jude Kelly's visit Robin Hutchinson and I went to talk to Peter Hall about our plans and also to enlist his support for the adapted artistic policy. He was already associated with Kingston, having become Chancellor of Kingston University in 2000 and a Vice-President of the appeal. We met Hall in the middle of the morning in a secluded bar close to the Haymarket Theatre, where he was preparing a production of Oscar Wilde's *Lady Windermere's Fan* with Vanessa Redgrave, Redgrave's daughter Joely Richardson and David Yelland. He had seen the Rose plans, of course, and had leant his name to our appeal. It quickly became evident that he had keenly anticipated our meeting: he said that not only did he support the idea of more in-house production work for a theatre which deserved new work, but that he 'would like to be involved'. For us, this evidently and immediately changed the nature of what we were doing. Peter was especially interested in the idea of the new theatre collaborating with the university and with its students. He recounted how he had been in talks with an American university about a role bringing together students studying with the work of a public theatre, but that for financial reasons and a recession the talks had stalled. So the seeds of his time as the first Artistic Director of the Rose were sown.

We chatted about our families: with six children, including four daughters, born over a period of thirty five years and four marriages he had more experience of fatherhood than I had with my four daughters, but we had similar worries wherever they were and whatever they were doing. Robin, as well, had two young children. It was Hall's daughter Rebecca who was his particular worry at that time: she was in her second year at Cambridge, but had announced her determination to leave before completing her degree on the grounds that she wanted to get on and into theatre. He was trying to persuade her to stay for her final year. She had, of course, some experience as an actor: as a ten year old she had played a leading role in her father's television production of *The Camomile Lawn* and was deeply involved with Cambridge drama. A Cambridge graduate himself, Hall joked about Americans asking him, 'What is the secret about Cambridge University Drama School that it produces so many actors and directors?' He would reply, 'It's secret is simple: it doesn't have a drama school'.

In the upshot, Rebecca had her way and left, but despite being thwarted by his daughter, Hall was not averse to a little nepotism: later that Autumn it was announced in the press that Rebecca Hall would make her West End stage debut in Peter Hall's production of Shaw's *Mrs Warren's Profession*, when she might otherwise have been finishing her degree. She would play Vivie, Mrs Warren's daughter, a major role for any young actress. Hers was a superb performance: her relaxed, lighthearted and engaging quality demonstrated a natural stage ability and she won the Ian Charleson Award for best newcomer. She would win further acclaim for her performance in her father's production of *As You Like It*, eventually seen at Kingston's Rose. A touch of familial patronage was theatre's gain! From another theatrical family, the young Laurence Fox, soon to become my brother's sidekick in ITV's *Lewis*, played Frank Gardner. With a further little piece of serendipity, when this same production of *Mrs Warren's Profession* left the Strand theatre on a national tour Hannah Yelland, who had contributed so much to our artistic review, succeeded Rebecca as Vivie Warren.

On our way back to Kingston that day, Robin and I had much to talk about. It was certainly a turn that we had not anticipated. We had set off that morning to get Hall's support for a particular approach to programming and it appeared that he was offering very much more. When

I had a call from Peter later that evening this sense was confirmed: he wanted to reemphasise how serious he was and could we meet again the following day. Over a cup of tea at the Garrick Club the next afternoon he said, 'I want to lead this and be your artistic director – if you'll have me'.

I was delighted, of course, but also felt an underlying ambivalence: there was a nagging sense – probably because I had envisaged something rather different – that our aspirations to be new and groundbreaking might be compromised. Peter Hall's work had had a fundamental influence on me: my father had taken me to Stratford in June 1965 to see Hall's great *Henry 1V* productions – part of his seven history plays cycle – and also *Hamlet* with David Warner. I can remember still the physical sensation, not only of the sight of the dramatic action, but hearing Shakespeare's language; that Stratford experience had a lasting impact on my life and career. But equally, images of the experimental theatre of the ilk of Complicité or Kneehigh would possibly have to be shelved at least temporarily. I think Robin saw the practical reality of the kudos the project would win with Peter to the fore: in this respect, Robin was unencumbered. As time went on, I think our positions changed as I became wedded to Peter's vision and Robin maintained a more critical detachment.

Peter Hall's appointment as Artistic Director, which began to be formalised early in 2003, potentially fulfilled our ambition that Kingston's new theatre would make an impact well beyond the immediate vicinity of the town. He was to be paid a salary by KTT and this would be enhanced by Kingston University as he would become Professor of Drama. However, whilst his contract emphasised many obvious areas of service and commitment, there was one which stood out as the theatre's pressing need: Peter would act as 'the principal figurehead for the fundraising campaign'. As early as our meeting at the Garrick, Peter had insisted that the one thing he was not very good at was fundraising, but it was a warning we chose to treat as a self-deprecating caveat.

Peter led the publicity drive, with his ease making public pronounce-ments: 'This is the acting space and auditorium,' he said, 'that I have been dreaming of all my life. It is intimate, yet epic ... the use of the ground plan of Shakespeare's first theatre, the Rose, allied to modern building techniques has been a stroke of genius. It is a modern theatre which has all the strengths of the past'. Of course, the Rose was, strictly speaking, not Shakespeare's first theatre, nor *his* theatre at all. The Theatre, the Globe and, later, Blackfriars were far more central to his work. Possibly, *Henry VI Part 1* was played in the Rose and certainly, as Henslowe records in his *Diary* in February 1593, *Titus Andronicus*. There may have been others and, perhaps, he acted at the Rose, but scholars are divided. However, it was the choice of those two words 'intimate' and 'epic' which was so telling and apposite and they are the qualities which the Rose has and, so long as no one meddles with it, will always have.

Peter Hall was well-qualified to speak and we listened. In a career which began at Windsor in 1953 his achievements were formidable, especially in establishing great theatres and companies. It was his response to one play, a play which really established him as a significant practitioner, that best demonstrates his theatrical character. Hall's production of *Waiting for Godot* opened at the Arts theatre in 1955. Beckett's play was not then the timeless classic that it has become, but Peter recognised in it something others had missed: of Beckett and his play Hall said, 'Here was a voice, a rhythm, a shape that was very particular: lyrical, yet colloquial; funny yet mystical. Though expressed in natural speech, unpretentious and believable, it was much *more* than natural speech: there was a haunting sub-text'. From that point onwards, Hall's career became characterised by productions drawn from the classical repertoire and of new plays which he felt would stand the test of time: it had to be good text. So Aeschylus, Sophocles and Euripides were a constant source of inspiration. Shakespeare was his Emperor, but he relished Wilde and Shaw, Chekhov and Ibsen. Many modern playwrights owe him a debt: Pinter, perhaps the foremost, but also Hare, Ayckbourn, Whiting, Albee, Tennessee Williams, Edgar and Shaffer amongst many other (mainly male) authors. Apart from Pam Gems' *Piaf*, Timberlake Wertenbaker's *Gallileo's Daughter* and his wife Nikki Frei's translation of Feydeau's *Where There's a Will* (and later her adaptation of Henry James's *The Portrait of a Lady*) he had rather neglected female playwrights as a director, despite including Caryl Churchill's *Cloud Nine* in his 1997 season at the Old Vic – directed not by Hall, but by Tom Cairns. Perhaps the new millennium, the new wave of female writers and the new theatre in Kingston would see Peter Hall direct more work by women.

If he was reticent with regard to female playwrights, the same cannot be said of his response to actresses: early in his career he directed Edith Evans who had, he liked to remind us, learned her verse speaking from the great nineteenth century director, William Poel, whom Peter considered as a sort of forefather of his own approach to Shakespeare. He would talk of Edith Evans with a reverence not given to the great actors – Gielgud, Olivier, Laughton, Scofield, Finney – who were, nevertheless, routinely members of his casts and who had his respect. Over the years, our finest actresses had been enormously loyal to Hall: Vanessa Redgrave, Judi Dench and on to the younger generation of those like Felicity Kendal and Janie Dee. He drew, it seems, something special from the women he worked with. Of the great Peggy Ashcroft he wrote: 'Throughout my career, her belief in me gave me strength. It was never more important than in 1959, at the start of the RSC'. This, of course, is a reference to his first great and lasting achievement: the establishment of the Royal Shakespeare Company. Later he would succeed Olivier as artistic director of the National Theatre and lead it, at last, to its permanent home on the South Bank. At the same time, he was directing opera at many of the world's leading opera houses – the Royal Opera House, New York's Metropolitan Opera, Bayreuth with a celebrated production of Wagner's *Ring Cycle*; and, finally, as artistic director of Glyndebourne Festival Opera from 1984 (whilst still running the National Theatre) until 1990.

Harold Pinter said of Hall, at the time of his appointment to Kingston, 'Peter's a remarkable man of the theatre. He's a phenomenon. I don't know anybody with such enthusiasm, energy and stamina'. Nicholas Hytner, newly installed at the National following the regimes of Hall, then Richard Eyre and Trevor Nunn, said, 'His breadth of taste, his buccaneering support of the new and disreputable, his nose for talent, his faith in the ability of others: they are all inspirations to me'. On the face of it, we had come up trumps! Robin Hutchinson and I had to pinch each other all over again.

13
Planning and Performance

The theatre had by now become known as the Rose. Harold Pinter said it should be 'Rose of Kingston' – giving it personality, interest and other things besides (including this book's title). Michael Billington wrote: 'Rose of Kingston – it sounds, as one dramatist tartly observed, like a pub or a local lady of pleasure'. And so she became, for quite some years. I was sorry when it defaulted to *the* Rose Theatre, Kingston, but needs of branding and publicity apparently demanded it.

Peter Hall would be coming to Kingston, but there were many details to resolve before the public announcement. In the meantime, we had the excitement of our first performances in the theatre – our 'Season in the Shell' – to look forward to in March 2003. St. George had assured us that the shell would be completed by the end of 2002, but that we could go ahead with a 'Theatre Professionals Day' on 25th November. It was the first occasion that theatre practitioners from across the country had the opportunity to see what was happening. Barrie Rutter had asked if he could say a few words: the following Spring he was to be the first professional actor to step onto the stage as the Chorus in his own production of *Henry V*. I had shown the plans to Barrie a couple of years previously: we had met at the Wilde Centre, Bracknell before his performance as Falstaff in his Northern Broadsides production of *The Merry Wives of Windsor*. On that occasion he looked carefully at the drawings, muttering in his uncompromising Yorkshire: 'It's good, this is ... I like that ... ', before looking up and holding me with those dangerous eyes of his. 'There aren't any fucking pillars, are there?' No, I said, no pillars. 'Good job!' He went on to tell me that he'd recently done 'a residency' at the new Shakespeare's

Globe, '... and someone's put some pillars right in the way. You don't want pillars there!'

Two years later on that chill November day in the Rose shell, he stood on the stage, his eyes gleaming. 'I'm Barrie Rutter', he said, as though anyone there needed to be told. 'We're bringing a couple of plays here in March, *Henry Five* and *A Woman Killed with Kindness*. We've got a set. We'll bring it in, we'll put it down, we'll look at it, we'll probably take it straight back out again!' His voice warmed with his enthusiasm: 'You don't *need* anything in here. The building's done it for you! And look ...' (I'd put a fire extinguisher at the back of the top level in the auditorium, its red standing out from the concrete) '... I can nearly touch the furthest person in the audience. And best of all, there's no – pillars!" Few knew why he had hesitated over that final word.

There was a moment after the meeting had finished, when it was dark outside and everyone was leaving the building. A figure, like a Russian countess dressed in fur hat and coat, was moving around the back concrete lower auditorium and calling in a resonant and commanding voice, 'Am I too late? Have you finished?' It was Janet Suzman, who had as she said, 'Got my buses wrong' and been delayed. She had time and enough light to see the space. 'Oh yes!' she said. 'This *is* good!' If the afternoon did nothing else, it began to place the voice of the actor – and great actors, to boot – into Kingston's Rose.

We repaired to whatever was where Brown's Restaurant now is on Charter Quay to give Janet a cup of tea and to listen to her and Peter Hall reminisce about plays done and to talk of plays to come. There was a real sense of optimism by the Thames that afternoon.

Optimism was a feeling not shared less than 150 miles to the north-west in Worcester, where the Swan Theatre, another Elizabethan namesake, was preparing to close its doors as a professional producing house after its local council ignored the social and economic arguments about investment in the arts and withdrew its support. As our determination in Kingston developed to become a major producing theatre, the closure of the Swan in January 2003 meant that there was no producing theatre between Birmingham and Bristol. Fortunately, in Kingston's Guildhall there were now some rather more enlightened local authority thinkers.

The 'Season in the Shell' was designed to build involvement and expectation, as well as to herald the campaign to raise funds for the fit out. It would celebrate the space, showing how unique it was and embracing people into it. We wanted the Arts Council, National Government, the Local Authority, the local community and local businesses to sit up and take notice. To coincide with the Spring Season, we planned a debate centering on the arts as a socially regenerative force which would provide another focus point for journalists and the public at large. The Theatre Management Committee, running affairs since the building of the shell began, met in early December.

We were challenged – not for the first time, nor the last – by funding problems: the building needed to be brought up to standard for public use in order to get a licence for the season. The work required would not necessarily mean progressing the building towards completion. Michael Holden revealed that an estimated £395,000 of building work was needed to ensure the Spring Season could happen and approximately £95,000 of this would have to be written off after the season – nearly half as much again as the figure he had given to us in November. This work was due to begin in mid-January, but with no guarantee that it would be finished in time. We were confronted with a number of options, one of which was to cancel the Spring Season altogether. It was a distinctly tricky position to be in, yet it would be untenable to cancel as credibility and confidence would collapse: our job as a Trust was to promote theatre. Equally, a loss of £95,000 would be impossible to justify with the coffers lacking coinage, and there was still the problem that there was no guarantee of completion. Holden was asked to review how we could proceed with less building work (for instance, by reducing the audience capacity) and a lower write-off sum. We would meet again in a matter of days, whilst the interim would give most of us furrowed brows by day and sleepless nights. Less than a week later, on an evening abutting Christmas, we were able to ratify a basic programme of building to accommodate a smaller audience. The financial loss, those tendering for the work would be told, must not exceed £50,000. In addition, the TMC was reassured by Holden that the works would be done in time for the Spring Season.

In early January we felt more confident. Gail Cunningham, chairing the TMC, reasserted our ambition as she stressed that the Spring Season would go ahead and that it was the first opportunity to demonstrate the uniqueness of the space, locally, nationally and internationally. We also wanted to show how the theatre could begin to transform Kingston at night: the attractive mediaeval market town by day had become a rather challenging and not-altogether friendly location after dark, even in the centre, in fact especially in the centre. Nocturnal rejuvenation was an important objective and one that was shared across the political spectrum.

Gail and I had another national and international appointment on Saturday 15th February, along with millions. Before mid-day we waited with our partners and friends on the concourse of a seething Waterloo Station. During the hour or so we were there one of my daughters, Martha, called over from a part of the crowd moving at a different pace. Another daughter, Pip, made a call by mobile phone from Barcelona, where she was on the fringes of another vast crowd. We were a part of the largest political demonstration in British history and the largest coordinated demonstration across the world. By the time our group reached Hyde Park nearly four hours later, others on the London march (official police estimate well in excess of 750,000; BBC estimate well over a million; official march organisers' estimate 3 million; retrospective survey at least 2 million) were leaving, the speeches all having ended. The march failed, of course, to prevent the creation of the theatre we were so opposed to: the tragic theatre of war in Iraq.

In early 2003 there was a variety of theatre to occupy me alongside my drama teaching and theatre research at the University and our committee work at the Rose. For many years I had spent enjoyable Januaries involved with a charity pantomime, initiated by Robin Hutchinson and Lesley Hawkes and still now a regular feature of the Tolworth Cornerhouse repertoire. This year, I played Big Horse in *The Lone Stranger*, an adaptation of whatever we did the year before and the year before that (Dixon in *Dixon of D'Arcy Green* and a mad scientist in *2001, A Space Oddity*).

Meanwhile, in more mainstream theatre, Trevor Nunn's swansong in charge of the National Theatre was a wonderful *Anything Goes* and

– for me the pick of the year – Greg Doran's Elizabethan, Jacobean and Caroline season of RSC Swan Theatre productions, which transferred to the Gielgud and included terrific productions of *The Malcontent*, *Eastward Ho!*, *Edward 1V* and *The Roman Actor*.

In an occasional diary I noted on the 5th February, one of my university courses, *Shakespeare: Yesterday, Today and Tomorrow* began and 'thank goodness to be teaching'. It was always my first love, professionally. This term had some interesting moments: Hannah Yelland came in to talk about *Mrs Warren's Profession*, having replaced Rebecca Hall for the national tour. One morning Peter Hall himself came into one of my classes; we were exploring the rhythms in the iambic line so he quickly took the opportunity to take over and keep the students enraptured for an hour and a half.

The Season in the Shell was planned for March. We engineered a temporary performance licence and from a talented shortlist chose Phil Willmott, the brilliant award-winning director and composer, to devise and direct a community play. Then Barrie Rutter would lead Northern Broadsides – no strangers to 'found' spaces and empty warehouses – in *Henry V* and *A Woman Killed With Kindness*. Temporary seating, heating and lighting were installed and a novel feature would be 'groundlings' standing in the pit.

Phil Willmott conceived *Don Juan In Kingston*. Local lawyers and business women, resting actors and factory machine operators, shop staff and secretaries were soon rehearsing with university students and school children in a coming together of the Kingston community. The plot was simple, as the pre-production puff advertised:

> When Don Juan, the greatest lover of all time, is cornered by a mob of vengeful husbands in sixteenth century Spain, he sends up a prayer for his patron saint to rescue him. The mischievous deity transports him across time and space and dumps the Spanish nobleman and his servant in modern day Kingston! The fun really starts when Don Juan enlists the help of the neighbourhood's women to make his new tapas bar a success; he soon

discovers that modern day romance works somewhat differently! Undeterred and with a little help from the local community – including the pub next door, a Korean parade, a karaoke machine and four passing angels – he soon has the whole of Kingston singing and in love with life! Packed with favourite pop songs, action, comedy and romance …

Kingstonians John Hackett and Amanda Shaw were the first male and female players to speak dialogue on the Rose stage, and so the building came to life. Roger Hayes, then Leader of the Council, brought political edge to the role of Don Carlos. Over one hundred volunteers were involved. There were no auditions as Willmott gleefully took all-comers: 'My main objective', he said, 'was to get as many people on stage as possible, claiming the theatre as their own'. Willmott used some of the theatre's features effectively, notably the galleries above the stage, where musician Mike Greenway had his band of keyboards, guitars, oboe and drums. It was a colourful and joyous production, with wittily adapted pop songs, and – with more than a nod to Gloria Gaynor – 'We Will Survive' struck a note of determination that, having come this far, Kingston's theatre would finally open in fully fitted-out fashion.

The following week Barrie Rutter brought his company to the stage, with Conrad Nelson playing King Henry. They alternated *Henry V* with Thomas Heywood's domestic tragedy *A Woman Killed with Kindness*. Rutter said of his Broadsides repertoire that there was a 'sweet circularity' in coming to Kingston's Rose. Shakespeare's *Henry V* had been one of the first productions at the new Globe Theatre which Richard Burbage's company had established in 1599, close to – and so in competition with – the original Rose. More appositely still, *A Woman Killed With Kindness* was quite possibly one of the last plays to be seen at the Elizabethan Rose, being performed there in early 1603, the year of the original Rose's demise and the monarch's death.

Rutter's performance as Chorus in *Henry V* suggested an immediate and instinctive understanding of how the new Rose might work, an understanding which has not always been replicated by others down the years.

There were oratorical flourishes, but there were also moments when he drew the audience to him, making them complicit in the anticipated action and, crucially, recruiting them to the creative process:

> ... Can this cockpit hold
> The vasty fields of France? Or may we cram
> Within this wooden O the very casques
> That did affright the air at Agincourt?
>
> ...
>
> And let us, ciphers to this great account,
> On your imaginary forces work.
> Suppose within the girdle of these walls
> Are now confined two mighty monarchies,
> Whose high upreared and abutting fronts
> The perilous narrow ocean parts asunder:
> Piece out our imperfections with your thoughts;
>
> ...
>
> For 'tis your thoughts that now must deck our kings,
> Carry them here and there; jumping o'er times,
> Turning the accomplishment of many years
> Into an hour-glass.

Rutter was the storyteller and when he urged the audience, the night before the Battle of Agincourt, 'Now entertain conjecture of a time ... ', it was as though he was prompting each person watching *individually* to be there. In this great Shakespearean epic he created moments of intimacy: it made for exciting and interactive theatre.

The production had been reviewed before it arrived in Kingston. Lyn Gardner, Guardian theatre critic and Kingston resident, had written: 'Conrad Nelson's Henry is no cut-out hero, but a man struggling to find himself and desperately wanting. Like all the other performances here it is strong, direct and feels scrupulously honest. It is acting without the fancy show-off bits, and you can't help warming to it'. Of both Broadsides productions Michael Coveney said in the *Daily Mail*, 'The spirit of national grit and glory suggested by the Shakespearean tradition of strolling players is best embodied today by Northern Broadsides ... An Elizabethan double of special quality ... here is the true, beating heart of British theatre'. We hoped that it would rub off on the Rose.

There had been two potentially ill-starred incidents on Tuesday 18th March, the opening night of *Henry V.* A sense of expectation was evident as a large audience, wrapped in overcoats against the chill, listened to the opening salvoes. Shortly before the interval, the English forces are at the walls of Harfleur and Rutter, clearly relishing the occasion as the Chorus, completed his speech, the confidante of the audience:

> Suppose the ambassador from the French comes back;
> Tells Harry that the king doth offer him
> Katharine his daughter, and with her, to dowry,
> Some petty and unprofitable dukedoms.
> The offer likes not: and the nimble gunner
> With linstock now the devilish cannon touches,
>
> And down goes all before them. Still be kind,
> And eke out our performance with your mind.

He had lowered his voice for the final line and a half and, with his eyes blazing and holding the audience, he moved backwards to the exit stage left. As he moved out of the subdued light the edge of the stage tapered upstage and, missing his footing, he fell backwards landing on the bannister of the steps leading up from the Pit, it seemed in slow motion. He rolled off the bannister and slipped into the wings. Many would not have noticed as his fall coincided with an explosion of cannon fire. I slipped backstage to find him being attended to by my old university friend, Mel Howley from Halifax, who was working with Northern Broadsides. Barrie was clearly in pain, but my concern was met with an expletive, indicating that he would just get on with it.

By then we had reached the interval and I went round to the concrete steps to our temporary office, to find Peter Hall being attended to having tripped and fallen down the steps. He had a gash on his head. Like Rutter, he brushed it aside and was soon, with a glass of red wine in hand, talking about the technical details of the stage and its effects. I hoped, with a flickering of superstition, that neither accident would prove inauspicious.

The images in the theatre and beyond following performances of *Don Juan In Kingston*, *Henry V* and *A Woman Killed With Kindness* remain with me: the colour and spectacle of over a hundred performers on the stage singing in celebration; audience members talking avidly in the as yet unheated, unfinished bar, smiles on their faces; the intensity of concentration in the auditorium as one of the country's finest touring groups played two classical works, already lauded in the national press; the local restaurants filling with punters; great figures from the world of theatre affirming that Kingston had built a fine theatre of the future; the groundlings in the pit relishing contact with the action; the sound of sustained applause at the end of every one of the ten performances; people of all ages wandering through the centre of Kingston after 10.30pm, theatre programmes tucked under their arms.

We emerged from the Spring Season with a lower net loss – somewhere just over £20,000 – than anticipated which, considering the structural work needed, was encouraging. We had not drawn down from the RBK loan of £900,000 yet, but inflation was creeping up towards 6%, with a prediction of a rise as high as 9%. The first thing to be hit would be building costs and without substantial funds coming into the Appeal and a delay over re-design the situation would continue to be uncertain. Peter Hall's imminent appointment meant that the business plan would require considerable adjustment and it would inevitably affect the fit-out plans too.

On Friday 21ˢᵗ March, during the Northern Broadsides run, Kingston University, the Royal Borough and the Theatre Trust collaborated on a half-day conference called 'Creativity, Culture and Regeneration'. The conference was chaired by Bruce Macdonald, RBK's Chief Executive and speakers included Sir Peter Scott, the University's Vice Chancellor and also Sir Peter Hall, soon to become officially Artistic Director. Thus, it underlined the strength of the partnership engaged on building the Rose and also drew further national limelight to what was happening in Kingston.

Bruce Macdonald's opening remarks set the tone: 'The Royal Borough of Kingston is delighted to be working with Kingston Theatre Trust and with Kingston University to bring forward this conference. We all have a shared interest in the theatre and in culture generally – both of which are powerful catalysts within community ... There are economic, cultural and social factors which interact with each other to promote a thriving community'. He concluded: 'Culture should be regarded as part of the fabric of our town, rather than a decorative addition'. Robin Hutchinson spoke with fervour about the value of dreaming and fulfilling a dream, of the regenerative values of the Baltic Centre in Gateshead, of the Lowry in Salford and Tate Modern in London, but he also offered a word of caution: 'We don't want to arrive at a point, in twenty years time, where a lot of these community ventures are floundering because they weren't embedded in an environment with its own artistic, creative and cultural energy'. The reference to the Tate Modern was a cue to Fred Manson, an international expert on regeneration, who applauded the fact that a project of such significance was driven at local level and without going to the national government.

I was especially looking forward to what Lyn Gardner, of *The Guardian*, would have to say. She was speaking especially about theatre outside theatre building, theatre on the street. A year earlier, she had written critically about the building of our theatre as 'misplaced civic pride'. At the professionals' day in the Autumn Jude Kelly had made a point of speaking to her and then in January – a couple of months before the conference – I had met her for coffee on Charter Quay and she said she was changing her mind: 'I still think you are mad, but what can I do to help?' She had promised then to get a *Guardian* contact for the conference, but turned up herself to give a paper, arguing for theatre to take to the streets. She asserted, 'I think this theatre could make a major contribution to Kingston, but it should be something which moves out of this ticket selling theatre into the lovely little spaces immediately outside – on the riverfront and through to the market itself '. It's what the International Youth Arts Festival, now Fuse International, has done particularly to fulfil this aspiration.

Peter Hall affirmed much that had been said, but added, 'I'd like to talk about one thing you left off during earlier presentations today: social regeneration – fine; physical regeneration – fine. But I would like to put up front spiritual regeneration ...' and he gave the argument a universal twist: "If I had to bring up my children, limited to one particular section of past culture, I would choose theatre. There are a thousand plays which teach you how to live. Drama doesn't say go out and kill each other, go out and steal, go out and lie, go out and cheat; drama is essentially moral, and it asks a great big question: "how can we be moral?" '

Sir Peter Scott, the University's Vice Chancellor, was one of a handful of people at the conference who knew of Hall's imminent appointment as Artistic Director. He agreed with Hall that there might be difficulties ahead, but offered this reassurance: 'I'd like to tell you that the University will remain committed, absolutely committed, to this project.' He was aware of some of the pejorative suggestions: that this theatre was being built to satisfy some Victorian sense of pride, but Scott challenged this saying that the University *does* consider that it has a civic role: '... civic in the best sense, relating to civil society and ideas of citizenship, emancipation and enlightenment'. He brought together a sense of the value of creativity, intellectual engagement and imagination, drawing the conference to a conclusion: 'The last thing I want to say is that universities, like theatres, are about making creative spaces in which people can let their imaginations roam. They're about intellectual imagination as much as creative imagination. They have a great deal in common, as in both cases they are essentially about trying to *imagine* other worlds, and then trying to *make* those other worlds – because you can't make another world without imagining it in the first place'.

The conference closed on that note.

14
Plans For Pilgimages

2003 was a time for change at the top of the two national companies: Michael Boyd would take over the RSC later in the year bringing to an end Adrian Noble's difficult time. Boyd's RSC tenure was to be transformative and included a resurgence in quality of productions in Stratford. It would also see the development of plans for a new main theatre. Meanwhile, at the National Theatre, Trevor Nunn's departure saw the installation of Nick Hytner who was to preside over a blockbusting opening season: *Jerry Springer – the Opera*, *Henry V* with Adrian Lester, and Michael Frayn's *Democracy*.

In Kingston we were appointing Peter Hall, who had founded the RSC and was the first director of the National Theatre when it finally moved into its Southbank home. He kept a wary and not always uncritical eye on his two theatrical progeny, as he did on his own tribe. I remember at one meeting in Kingston's Guildhall he produced the new National Theatre programme 'hot from the press'; Hall added, with some paternal pride, 'and the other bit of news is that my son [Edward] is to be Associate Director'.

Hall's appointment as Artistic Director was confirmed in June 2003 and, after twenty years of campaigning and developing on our part, it should have proved auspicious. It was made possible by the Kingston Theatre Trust, the Royal Borough of Kingston and Kingston University coming together and working with imagination and a little daring. Peter created a manifesto which he called 'A Theatre for the Future', which demonstrated how important it was that the principal stakeholders, the University and RBK, worked with his and the Trust's vision. The pay-off for each would be very considerable. There would be a 'crack theatre company', an ensemble of some dozen actors 'dedicated to producing work of the highest quality, both classical and modern, which will rank in the forefront of international theatrical activity'. The theatre would be 'at the cutting edge of new forms, new techniques and contemporary drama, as well as the re-energiser of classical techniques and traditions'. Heady stuff! We wanted to have wide audience appeal and also broaden the age range and cultural diversity. Of course, one can hear in this not only a vision translated into words, but also an anticipation of an appeal for arts funding as well as anticipation of criticism. Remembering it now, however, it rekindles the excitement I felt then and, that it was never entirely realised, by so much is the regret.

The University's interest in the theatre was in the stimulation of a research and development programme and a training which was, at the time, a unique idea. Peter and I would develop a two year post graduate training programme: students would learn from and in harmony with the actors in the theatre company and during the second year would become members of the company. Hall said himself in a press interview: 'The idea of having the Master of Fine Arts degree for actors and directors and designers and in their last year working in the company [seems] to me very exciting. There is nowhere in this country where somebody can train to be an actor and then, on the result they've achieved, move into a professional situation as part of the course'.

Hall had always considered himself in part as a teacher. He was now energised by the success of his book *Shakespeare's Advice to the Players*, recently published by James Hogan of Oberon Books. His thesis was simple: Shakespeare tells the actor everything she or he needs to know.

We spent hours, days, weeks, evenings, Sundays and suppers planning the course and the means by which it could be integrated into the work of the theatre. By this time, the drama programme at the university was flourishing as an undergraduate course and it was time to develop postgraduate work: this could be another flagship. I was fortunate to have some remarkable people in the university supporting and facilitating this, not least my own Dean, Gail Cunningham, now also a trustee. When Gail had asked the Vice Chancellor, Peter Scott, if the university could contribute substantially in support of Hall's appointment, his response was immediate: of course it would; it would not deserve to be a university if it did not. Scott was as good as his word.

The press was quick to respond to Hall's appointment: Charles Spencer wrote in the *Daily Telegraph*, 'Peter Hall, I suspect, could put Kingston on the map as a place of theatrical pilgrimage'. Hall himself made various media appearances, including on Radio 4's *Start the Week* and *Loose Ends*. These were the first of a series of programmes during the coming years which drew national attention to the theatre, culminating in a two part *South Bank Show* with Melvyn Bragg, some of it filmed in the Rose, celebrating Hall's fifty years in theatre.

In April 2003, an estimate was made that we needed something in the region of £3.25 million to complete the fit-out of the Rose theatre, a figure to which an equipment bill would need to be added. Our assumption of moving smoothly towards an opening was to be thwarted, but we began to make appointments. Sue Higginson, then Head of the National Theatre Studio, was to be the Rose's Executive Director. She had long been a collaborator with Hall, having assisted him with the transfer of the National Theatre from the Old Vic. She had returned to the National when the Studio was set up, initially under the directorship of Peter Gill, and she took over from him. Higginson's appointment was probably premature, but Hall insisted. During the first two months following the announcement of Hall's appointment, the Appeal realised £30,000, a rate of progress that would have to increase substantially should we be in a position to complete the fit-out on time for an opening in late 2004. Peter had, after all, said on the day we met at the Garrick that he was not very good at raising money, that he did not attract it. If we took it as false modesty then, the next three years and more would bring headaches and frustrations aplenty, as we struggled to maintain even enough to keep the project alive.

There were other tensions. While he was still on board, Michael Holden pressed us to continue the fit-out. However, with a new and evolving artistic policy and with Peter Hall as the theatre's principal (and not Michael) it was important to assess the designs. And the Spring

Season, too, had prompted thoughts about how the theatre might work in practice.

Rosie Hoare – fresh from her triumphant management of the building of the London Eye and calmly resolving problems there – would now manage the fit-out as Project Manager and the design would be taken on by Alison Chitty, the distinguished stage designer. Both Alison and Sue Higginson were awarded the OBE for services to theatre during the year. To complete a team of impressive talent with an international reputation, Paul Groothuis would oversee the sound system and Peter Mumford the lighting. It was, given a fair financial wind, a dream theatre team!

This, inevitably, meant that Michael Holden would leave the project. He had been working for several months in the knowledge that we had moved in a direction with which he was not comfortable. For five years Michael was a significant force in bringing this beautiful theatre to Kingston. I think that he had probably hoped to be the person to oversee the theatre into its first years of operation – as he had done as Chief Executive of the Globe. In some ways, he wanted to own too much and to take the project where he wanted it to go. He was something of a loner, but also someone who combined his fierce energy with a breadth of knowledge of different aspects of theatre structure and theatre-making from which Kingston benefited fundamentally.

The first feature to change was that the pit standing space disappeared. The Season in the Shell was the first and only time that a significant part of the audience stood. I was disappointed when the floor was raised: I found, as I do at the Globe, that there is an increased energy between the pit and the stage when the punters are on foot. There were times during the Season in the Shell when people left their seats after the interval to join the groundlings in the Pit. However, it is also true that some plays and productions work better than others in this regard. The muscularity of an Elizabethan or Jacobean playwright's language is more suited to this sort of interaction than, say, Chekhov's dialogue and action. The practical difficulty is that, whilst it would be possible to alternate between sitting and standing, it would take a team of technicians a day or more to effect the change in either way. Subsequently, of course, sitting on the floor in front of the stage has given way, in turn, to front stalls seating. There'll be no going back!

Morale remained high in the community: the Friends had grown in strength to 1500 following the opening season. During the preceding year they had raised over £50,000. The Friends' success was a great indication of their dedication and also the leadership of Roger Chown, along with his team which included Diana Robertson, Katie Worsley, Sue Moller, Lis Barrett, Katie Randerson, Jennie Matthew, Martin Higgs, Brian Creese and a host of others. Sue Higginson, shortly after her own appointment as Executive Director, said she had never seen anything quite like the Friends: she was 'knocked out'! The strength of the Friends remained an enormous source of confidence and they were to develop into one of the most important bodies of the completed Rose – the Volunteers – without whom it could not function and to whom this book is dedicated.

Another important annual event which had enriched the cultural life of Kingston and with which the developing theatre felt a close association was the Kingston Readers' Festival. The brainchild of Sandy Williams who continued to organise it year by year and worked with Herculean energy, it was supported, as Patron, by the world-renowned children's novelist and Kingstonian Jacqueline Wilson. Each year, having covered its costs, Sandy would hand over a cheque to the Theatre Friends. The Readers' Festival demonstrated that significant people from literature and the arts would come to Kingston and that there was an appetite for culture. Beryl Bainbridge, Alexander McCall Smith, Claire Tomalin, Julian Fellowes, Simon Hoggart, Tony Benn were a reflection of the many novelists, historians, biographers, script-writers, journalists and politicians attracted every year by the indefatigable Williams.

Raising money was now the preeminent imperative. With this in mind, Bernie McDermott, who had been Development Director at the National Theatre from 1996 to 1999, was brought in to refocus efforts, with a three month contract. With the appointment of McDermott, Geoff Howard stepped away from the fundraising, having had just a few weeks with Peter Hall on board to promote the new case for the Theatre. Howard was retained for a further two years as Company Secretary, a role he continued in on a pro bono basis from 2005 until 2018.

On a visit to Kingston, Trevor Nunn said that with McDermott on the team we should expect a successful and speedy outcome – a confidence that, sadly, was misplaced. McDermott's initial assessment was that £2 million was needed in the short term, that it was possible to raise that figure, but that this could not be done before the second week of December 2003 when the decision to proceed with the fit-out must be taken – and about the time his contract would expire. Consequently, his aim was to win time for the project in order to allow an intense fundraising effort to take place in early 2004. In the meantime, he was pursuing two options: firstly, the obtaining of guarantees and, secondly, a capital loan facility with a commercial bank. Of course, that would call into question the responsibilities and liabilities of Trustees, which was to become a matter for constant review for a number of years.

At the beginning of 2004 McDermott sounded bullish, but the context seemed more like a china shop: hope centred on the response from one particular source, a Kingston Hill resident, enriched by generations of fans of the beautiful game betting throughout the season, where hopes for a very major donation had been hinted at and harboured for some time. The outcome was a cheque for £1000. The current figure required stood now at £4.5million in order to complete the fit out, including £1.5million for equipment. Costs were not static: tender prices for buildings had risen by 25% in the four years since the millennium and we had a growing staff budget to fund. Rosie Hoare felt that an October opening was still just possible, but only if building work could begin on schedule in March and progress at top speed. It was not her fault, nor owing to any lack of realism on her part, that her plans would be thwarted then and several times more before the theatre finally opened three and a half years late. We realised how much we were now relying on the work of Bernie McDermott. With his own contract extended, he aimed to complete his work by the opening date and to bring in sufficient money to fund operations along the way.

Along with our own determination, we were driven too by Hall's artistic vision and our confidence was nurtured by his experience: few others in theatre history could be said to be unique; of Peter it could. He had brought together an impressive team – Hall himself, Higginson, Hoare, Mumford, Groothuis, McDermott and, shortly, David Fletcher, the former financial director at the RSC. An impressive team – and an impressive payroll, especially without a constant source of income. Hall planned an exciting season of plays for the Autumn of 2004, which would precede an official opening in the following January. Firstly, and most enticingly was the world premiere of a new Ariel Dorfman play, which would then go to Bath the following Summer. Shaw's *Man and Superman*, Moliere's *Don Juan* and Timberlake Wertenbaker's *Galileo's Daughter*, all Bath Festival productions from 2004, would follow before December. For the official Theatre Opening in January, he proposed *Much Ado About Nothing*, a wry title given the time the theatre had been in the making. This would be in repertory with another play, as yet unspecified, from Trevor Nunn. It was tempting stuff and would, we thought, both attract potential supporters, whilst immediately engaging students on our new postgraduate course, which was designed to be central to the theatre's working. Once open, the design team would disband, the fundraiser would depart and the payroll would be managed. Any delays, however, would be dangerously costly.

With a theatre executive now in place the Theatre Management Committee was dissolved. We had been actively driving the project for several years, whilst the Board met only from time to time. With the expectation of more rapid progress, the strategic and policy decisions would revert to KTT. I confess to being one of the optimists: I was particularly engaged both because the creation of the theatre had for over two decades been my aspiration and also, now, I had begun to create the innovative postgraduate training course with Peter Hall, who always mentioned the course in the same breath as the Rose itself. He saw this dual opportunity – running the Rose and teaching a new generation of theatre practitioners – as his last great contribution to theatre in this country, a life's work which led Michael Billington later to describe him in *The Guardian* as, 'the single most influential figure in modern British theatre'.

The March building deadline was missed, largely because funds had not materialised in any significant way. The next four years proved very difficult: we had a team of astonishing pedigree to fit-out and run our new theatre, but at every turn we were thwarted by a lack of money. Inevitably, tensions would develop and frustrations would begin to be aired. By July, McDermott reported feeble fundraising on a philanthropic basis and he was now pursuing an idea for a commercial company. RBK was, of course, kept in the picture and he began talking with the Borough about his plan.

Over the coming years, the Royal Borough – some of its senior officers and politicians – were to demonstrate a quality of engagement and commitment which remains admirable as an example of work in the public sphere. They were driven by a number of convictions: they were concerned for the developing wellbeing of Kingston and they took notice of the evident value of cultural regeneration and of the contribution that theatre can make to the economy of regions. However, it must be remembered that back in 1988 the Council had made a capital commitment of over £4 million to fund a theatre and recognised that there would need to be some revenue funding. The plan then was that the Kingston Theatre Trust would be asked to raise £1 million by appeal. The National Lottery, when it was created, was perceived as a let-out: it became the loophole which allowed the politicians of the early and mid-1990s to step aside, assuming funding would materialise from this new cash cow. The result was that the Trust was, by 2004, faced with raising over four times more than it was originally committed to, perhaps 60% of the total cost as opposed to less than 20%.

There was good evidence to hand for sharp-minded councillors and officers in RBK to support the theatre. In May 2004 the Arts Council published its most thorough report ever on the economic impact of UK theatre, a research survey run by Dominic Shellard of Sheffield University. Amongst some of its key findings was that, 'Theatre has a huge economic impact in this country – it is worth £2.6bn annually. The Wyndham Report, published in 1998, had established the contribution which West End theatres made to the London economy. This new report developed the detail of its predecessor in the context of London and reemphasised how the regions contribute in the national context: 'One of the key findings of the current study is that the combined impact of the 492 theatres outside London's West End is hugely important to the national economy'.

However, the 'convincer' for Kingston can be seen in one of the report's key conclusions:

> Each theatre makes both direct and indirect contributions to the
> local economy. The direct impact: local spending on purchasing
> supplies; wages paid to staff who live locally. The indirect impact
> is the 'knock-on' effect generated by the direct impact, where
> spending money leads to more money being spent. When
> theatres purchase supplies from a local company, that income
> helps the company pay wages to its staff who then use it to buy
> other goods. All that expenditure is constantly circulating around
> the local economy, helping to preserve jobs, and boost economic
> growth. The additional visitor spend also demonstrates how
> audience spending can make a significant difference to the
> local economy. By attracting people into an area - where they
> might eat out, spend money on transport or buy local produce -
> theatres help sustain jobs, generate additional economic activity
> and act as forces for economic and social regeneration.

The idea of economic and social regeneration as well as cultural
enhancement should, we believed, stop in their tracks the nay-sayers, the
whingers complaining of élitist diversion and those who would suggest that
for RBK to contribute meant depriving others. They became referred to,
after one particularly frequent contributor to the *Surrey Comet's* 'Letters to
the Editor' as 'the Scrubies of Berrylands'.

Amongst those who recognised the vital importance of preaching this
message directly to local commerce was Roger Chown. He had learned as
the leader of the early Friends' campaigns that there was an enthusiasm
in Kingston's business community. Now initially, he gave support to the
fledgling Development Department led by Matt Cull, but he then realised
there was more he could do personally. He left the Trust and joined the
staff of the theatre to focus on local businesses: he recalls Bob Cattaneo
of Cattaneo Professional Services saying, 'My business is the town and I
want to do my bit to help the Rose get off the ground'.

Obvious targets were restaurants, bars and cafés. The first big investment
came from John Scott, owner of the popular Frère Jacques restaurant on
Charter Quay, over several years offering a variety of substantial investments

and opportunities for theatregoers. On one occasion, when funds had dried up and David Fletcher came to Roger to say that five thousand pounds was needed to see the theatre through to the following day, Roger walked round to see Scott and returned thirty minutes later with a cheque. Commercial acumen mixed with philanthropy also motivated Russell-Cooke Solicitors, through John Hackett and Sarah Richardson, to sponsor the Friends for three years and the theatre in other respects, too. Not to be outdone, Carter Bells Solicitors gave generously at critical moments, as did Clear Insurance Management Group led by Howard Lickens. The CEO of the New Victoria Hospital, Charles Hutton, was a theatre-lover, but also believed there was an obligation to a business which considered itself a part of the town. Carluccios, Bentalls, John Lewis and others gave support in kind as well as financially, often at critical moments.

However, we needed some major money to complete the fitting-out and we were being drawn down the commercial company line. The idea was that RBK would transfer ownership of the building to a new company whilst retaining freehold of the land and having a 40% stake in the company. The company would licence KTT and its directors to manage the theatre, including its artistic programme and the Trust would pay a peppercorn rent. The company would own the theatre building, at that time valued at £2 million, and the fixtures which would be valued at £3.1 million, within a total fit-out cost of £6.4 million. The company would be valued at £5 million and the remaining £1.3 million of the fit-out cost would be raised philanthropically by KTT, as a registered charity. At the moment that Bernie McDermott laid out these plans to the Trust, he announced that he was having preliminary discussions with one particular individual, considering an investment of £2.5 million – a 50% stake. I remember my initial excitement being tempered immediately as Richard House asked a series of pertinent questions: would the asset of the Trust be diluted; would a return on investment be sought; what control would exist on how the business was run? It was much too early to say, came the reply. It is interesting to put House's questions into the context of the final outcome of these negotiations nearly two years later. In the meantime, we were sworn to secrecy that a deal was in the air and the name of the individual would be revealed at a later date.

Nadhmi Auchi was and is an interesting and not altogether uncontroversial character. His conviction for fraud – which he always contested – was reported in *The Guardian* on Saturday 15th November 2003, a few months before McDermott began negotiations with him:

> Mr Auchi, 65, was given a 15-month suspended sentence and a fine of €2m (£1.39m) on Wednesday at the end of the marathon corruption trial of former executives of the French oil company Elf. He was convicted – in what was France's biggest post-war corruption scandal – of accepting illegal commissions on the purchase of a Spanish oil refinery in the early 1990s on Elf's behalf and then handing back some of the money to the company's senior directors. Mr Auchi was originally arrested in London in April on a French extradition warrant issued two years ago. After his release, he voluntarily gave himself up to the French authorities. He told the court that because he was dealing with a state-owned company, he believed the transactions were above-board.

Reports in 2003 indicated he was one of the top ten richest people in Britain at the time – richer, it was said, than either Paul McCartney or the Queen!

In 2010 Auchi issued this statement as a footnote to a long article entitled *The Media: a reply to my critics* which he posted on his own website, the Nadhmi Auchi Foundation:

> On 12th November 2003 in the 11th Chambre Correctionelle du Tribunal in Paris I received a 15-month suspended sentence and a EUR two million fine after being found guilty of being an accessory to fraud. The charge related to the purchase of a Spanish-owned Kuwaiti oil company on behalf of Elf. I have consistently denied all wrong doing, believing that at all times I was acting with the knowledge of the French state and in the French national interest – as evidenced by the fact that at a breakfast meeting at the Elysée I received the personal thanks of

> President Mitterrand for my part in the transaction – one of the
> most profitable in Elf's history. I am continuing to appeal against
> the conviction and remain confident of a successful outcome.

The main article, to which this footnote is appended, is designed to rebut a swathe of allegations made about him at different times. Elsewhere he has had a better press: under a 2015 headline in *GMH News*, 'Billionaire Businessman Sir Nadhmi Auchi Believes in Giving Back', the opening paragraph runs:

> Some businessmen might make their fortune and invest it wisely;
> some might invest it unwisely; and still others of course might
> spend much it (*sic*). However, not all will choose to donate their
> money – or their time – to charitable and humanitarian causes.

It goes on to characterise Auchi as one of the latter. GMH is General Mediterranean Holding, Auchi's business holding company. There are reports of money raised for a variety of charities, for instance £35,000 towards the Kingston Hospital Cancer Unit.

In his own 'Full Biography' on the Nadhmi Auchi Foundation website, the Iraqi-born businessman lists two arrests and periods of imprisonment:

> Nadhmi joined the newly formed Baathist Party, attracted by its
> goals of pan-Arab unity, an end to the final vestiges of colonialism
> in the Middle East and economic equality. His activism led to his
> arrest in 1959 along with 76 other party members following a
> failed attempt to overthrow the government of Prime Minister
> Abdul Karim Qassim. Despite having only a minor and peripheral
> role, he was sentenced to three years 'rigorous imprisonment'.
> Following his release after two years, during which time he was
> beaten and tortured, Nadhmi Auchi left the Baathist Party to help
> form a new political grouping, the United Socialist Movement
> ... A year after the successful 1968 Baathist coup, Mr Auchi was
> arrested and imprisoned without trial by the new regime. He

resumed his career in 1969 and rose to become the Director of
Planning and Development at the Oil Ministry.

It hastens to point out that he left the country within a year of Saddam
Hussein becoming President of Iraq. This biography makes no reference
to his later problems with the French authorities.

His use of the title 'Sir' is, apparently, owing to his appointment in
late 2014 as Knight Commander of the Most Distinguished Order of the
Nation of Antigua and Barbuda. It is an honour awarded by those tropical
islands. An edition of the *Kingston Courier* in November 2016 carried
a story, also reported in the Caribbean press, about the honour being
withdrawn from both Auchi and another recipient: 'After discussions with
the United Kingdom's then-prime minister David Cameron, the Gover-
nor-General of Antigua and Barbuda, Sir Rodney Williams, wrote to
Mr Auchi, saying: "I am hereby withdrawing the honour bestowed upon
you until further notice". In that letter ... Sir Rodney told Mr Auchi:
"Some information has come to our attention suggesting that we do a
more detailed due diligence on some persons on whom honours have been
bestowed"'.

As far as KTT was concerned, Mr Auchi and General Mediterranean
Holding were a part of our hopes for funding from around July 2004 until
June 2006. During that time we had to fund the on-going project and pay
the salaries of our staff. The negotiations, which we had imagined would
move to a swift conclusion in 2004 seemed, in point of fact, interminable.
It was difficult to understand, assuming as we did that there was good
faith on both sides, why this should be.

It was at a meeting in October 2004 that we were finally vouchsafed
the name of our proposed investor. Bernie McDermott had, he said,
experienced problems in getting meetings to move plans on. The RBK
Chief Executive Bruce Macdonald assured us that Kingston remained
supportive, but that timing was critical. He also pointed out that RBK,
having created a 'gain' in the form of the shell, had a fiduciary obligation
to get something back for Kingston as well. A functioning theatre could
achieve that, but an empty shell could not. We also now began to feel
uneasy and there were questions which delay made more acute: there was

no indication of how KTT's role would develop within what now became known as 'Property Co' and later as the Kingston Theatre Property Company (KTPC). It was clear that separate fundraising would have to take place, even in the context of a successful outcome to the Auchi negotiations, in order fully to finance the fit-out. Our attempts in the philanthropic sphere remained obstinately unsuccessful.

The budget was beginning to look grim. In order to keep the Design team together until November and the Executive in place until January 2005 we would have to draw down on the RBK loan, leaving only a small amount – £30k – as a reserve. At that point Peter Hall and others had a face to face meeting with Mr. Auchi and were assured of his support: they were convinced by the handing over of a generous cheque for £50,000 to help the project into the New Year and further negotiations.

15
A Season in the Raw

The year 2004 was not all gloom. The Friends continued to demonstrate their great energy and now made a critical contribution which brought to the shell a production of international distinction, Peter Hall's first offering to the Rose.

Since their formation in May 2002 the Friends had grown around many imaginative events: open air entertainment at Dorich House, a Blues Night which realised £5000, the Season in the Shell Art Exhibition which raised £12,000, many quiz nights, leaflet drops, carols and concerts all of which had raised nearly £50,000 in a little over eighteen months. Whilst the professional fundraising efforts were becalmed, Roger Chown, Sue Moller and Katie Worsley launched their most ambitious project so far with an Auction of Promises. Sue Moller organised this evening at the Star and Garter, on Richmond Hill, and owing to the efforts of her team a generous profusion of items was given for auction, sale and tombola. From a Pete Townshend J-200 acoustic guitar, signed by Townshend, to lessons offered in English, Russian, Czech, Alexander Technique, Physics, to room design, to lunch with Ed Davey MP in the House of Commons, tea with Jacqueline Wilson at home or Janet Suzman at the Ritz, dinner with David Jacobs at the Garrick, to a Jerry Hall Christian Lacroix evening dress. Sport featured in golf with Ronnie Corbett, cricket bats from Alec Stewart, and a signed shirt from Martin Johnson who only months before had led England to their famous Rugby World Cup victory in Australia. There were opportunities to holiday in Cornwall, in the Pyrenees, in Mallorca. In all, there were 164 'lots' which raised £50,000 on that one evening. 'This will be a night to remember', said Sue Moller in the programme, and it was.

This success impinged directly on the theatre's future: a few months later, we decided that we must keep the artistic profile and potential rising. Hall offered to resurrect his successful Bath Festival production of *As You Like It* from the previous year. It would be a centrepiece of a 'Season in the Raw' which would play in the theatre from late November until mid-December. On successive Sundays during the run there would be two special events: *Judi Dench and Friends* on 5th December and *Jimmy Tarbuck and Friends* on 12th December. The shell had to be prepared for audiences and the season had to be underwritten, given the difficult situation we were in. The Friends were able to come to the rescue and so their Auction of Promises secured the season. The significance of this could not be underestimated and can be seen with a glance at the reviews for *As You Like It*:

> A Rose has bloomed sensationally in Kingston … an event of major importance to serious theatregoers … this brave new playhouse [has] an epic intimacy and a clear view with which other theatres of this size and scope cannot compete.
>
> Nicholas De Jongh,
The Evening Standard.

Before that, Hall had to revive his production and re-rehearse his cast. He wrote of that experience:

> I shall not easily forget Thursday, 18 November 2004. It was the first opportunity I had to rehearse my production of *As You Like It* on the stage of a new theatre – Rose of Kingston. The company ran through part one in the morning and, flushed with excitement, delivered part two in the afternoon. The stage didn't just work – it was a wonder. The actors found their voices and their feet with ease. I noticed immediately that Shakespeare's text, with all the demands it makes, was interacting perfectly with the shape of the stage.

All my life I have been telling actors that 'eyeball to eyeball'
acting, while perfect for naturalistic plays, simply does not work
when there is a 25-line speech to be delivered. The audience
feels left out. Although the speech may begin and end with the
actor speaking directly to another character, its main part, with
descriptive metaphors, puns and antitheses, and all the rest of
the Shakespearean vocabulary, inevitably has to be aimed at the
audience. They need to participate. Their imaginary forces must
be allowed to work.

The shape of the Rose stage in Kingston makes this process easy,
fluent and natural – but then, this could be expected, because it
is based on the ground plan of the stage where Shakespeare first
worked. It gave me the best day of rehearsal I remember in 50
years.

In the subsequent reviews both Hall and Kingston itself got a good press:
'The burly, indefatigable and often outspoken father figure of modern
British theatre ... has found a new berth in Kingston upon Thames', wrote
Charles Spencer in *The Daily Telegraph*. 'At the packed performance to
which reviewers were invited, with many students sitting on cushions
in the pit, there was no doubt that this is already a theatre that works
brilliantly.' Spencer saw the promise: 'This exciting new theatre, brimming
with potential, has got off to the best possible start and, with luck, should
be fully up and running by this time next year. Hall is enjoying a glorious
Indian summer as a director. At Rose of Kingston, we can anticipate a
blaze of wise, autumnal glory'.

It seemed that the two 'selling points' – the theatre and Peter Hall
– were doing their job and Benedict Nightingale in *The Times* sounded
pleased with himself and everyone else when he picked up on Hall's
intimate/epic trope: 'They have modelled their auditorium on the Rose
Theatre as excavations in the Southwark of 1989 revealed it to have been
four centuries earlier. Peter Hall was impressed enough to become the
theatre's first director. As his christening production shows, his judgment

is as good as ever ... It's intimate enough for the eroticism that fills *As You Like It* and epic enough for the battles that don't'.

Of course, the production of *As You Like It* had been reviewed in Bath eighteen months earlier, but the fact that all the national critics came to Kingston and offered such approval for the theatre was just what we wanted. For all the financial frictions, the theatre won accolades without reservation. Peter Hall had followed his disappointment that his daughter Rebecca had left Cambridge before taking her degree by casting her in *Mrs Warren's Profession*. Now, she played Rosalind, the role so memorable in the careers of many great actresses and perhaps most famously by Vanessa Redgrave at Stratford in 1961 at the age of twenty-four. Rebecca Hall was a year or two younger as she took on the role and Michael Billington had confessed in *The Guardian* to being 'smitten' when he saw her at Bath. He now wrote: 'Where some Rosalinds seem tiring company after a hard day in the forest, Hall's made you feel that her inability to declare her love was a source of spiritual frustration'. Billington, nevertheless, began to discuss the way more experienced actors began to adapt their performances to the space, something I will explore later. He concluded by saying, 'These are early days but already it is clear that the Rose is an exciting space and a magnificent opportunity'.

Pleasure was topped out by the success of the two '...*and Friends*' evenings. *Judi Dench and Friends* on Sunday 5th December 2004, was a unique theatrical experience with some of the nations finest actors. Samantha Bond, Alan Dobie, Rebecca Hall, David Oyelowo, Tim Pigott-Smith, Colin Salmon, Samuel West, Charles Dance, Julian Glover, Martin Jarvis, Michael Pennington, Dan Stevens and Harold Pinter (in actorly mode) joined the great Dame herself in a witty welcome to the theatre, performing monologues which made it seem the most classy series of auditions ever taken. The evening was devised by John Miller, directed by Joe Harmiston and included extracts from Margaret Attwood, JM Barrie, Samuel Beckett, Alan Bennett, Anton Chekhov, Noel Coward, Richmal Crompton, Charles Dickens, TS Eliot and William Shakespeare. The young also played: the Chicken Shed Theatre Company performed, the Tiffin School Choir was directed by Simon Toyne and I directed twenty five of my University students in an extract from *Murder in the Cathedral*

with Thomas Becket played by the young Ben Barnes, prior to his elevation
to the aristocracy as Prince Caspian.

The following Sunday Jimmy Tarbuck was accompanied by a host of
entertainers, including Cilla Black, Ronnie Corbett, Kenny Lynch, David
Jacobs himself, and two of The Moody Blues!

The Season in the Raw was an opportunity, too, to assess the whole
facility and the design plans inevitably changed. Two of the three
performance spaces – the main Rose auditorium and the Studio –
would be retained, although the so-called Education Room (the Creative
Workshop) would be given over to technical bases. There would,
potentially, be a third performance space: the Gallery would double as a
place for fine art and for the embodiment of drama. Robin Hutchinson,
a professional artist in one of his many guises, was disappointed to lose
the third space and to find the Gallery compromised, but he reluctantly
agreed that this was the best practical solution: we could not make new
productions in the theatre without some technical workshop space on site.

And so as 2005 dawned it was with a sense of auspicious progress. The
theatre worked well and had attracted audiences from very much further
afield than Kingston, the national critics had without exception admired
it and the actors had relished playing in it. It also brought Jerry Gunn to
the Rose for the first time as the Company Stage Manager of *As You Like
It* and then as Associate Producer for the two charity gala events. As the
theatre opened he was to become the General Manager and later, with
great distinction, Executive Producer for over a decade.

Alas, the fundraising effort seemed captivated, not by the positive
mood engendered by performance, but by the need to close the deal with
General Mediterranean Holding and its boss, Mr Auchi. At the December
meeting Auchi, it was said, would invest £3 million in the proposed
company. The offer was, apparently, conditional on Peter Hall continuing
as the theatre's director. He was also prepared to offer the balance required
for the full fit-out at an interest rate of 10% (the official bank rate was
moving down from 4.75% to 4.5 %). The theatre's operating plan should be
revised to demonstrate how KTT would work towards an annual dividend
of 5% on the investment. Needless to say, this felt distinctly uncomfortable
and both Richard House and David Errington pressed for more detail on

how such an arrangement would affect KTT, whilst Bruce Macdonald and Tony Knights were especially concerned quite rightly to protect a public asset. Prospects of an accommodation were inevitably bruised when the *Kingston Informer* scooped the news of the negotiations taking place and reminded readers of the Elf affair.

By April, delay had become seriously damaging and it was clear that negotiations were not running smoothly. The staff had to be put on notice. In June RBK again stepped in to keep the project afloat. Rosie Hoare by way of response – showing her unflappable and professional focus – quickly put in place a new plan which would see completion in August the following year. The RBK Executive Council decided to set up the Property Company immediately and take unallocated shares up to £750,000. They would underwrite a further £350,000 costs for fitting out, pending fundraising. £1.3 million worth of theatre equipment would be purchased and leased back to KTT at an initial £10,000 per annum, rising to £50,000 by year five. A new loan facility would be set up to allow the Trust to operate and a new Theatre Steering Group with RBK, Kingston University, KTT and Theatre Executive membership. General Mediterranean Holding could be represented if they so wished: it sounded a little non-committal! KTT released the design and fit-out works to the company to enable the principal objective of completing the theatre to be fulfilled, but such decisions only came after minute examination of proposals and often the Trust had to have legal advice to hand.

It was only on the GMH front that there was no apparent movement. David Fletcher had proved his worth with some detailed and complex work on behalf of KTT, work applauded by Tony Knights, RBK's Director of Finance. But by late September a document which most of us had expected to be ratified the previous July remained unsigned. Understandably, there were delays in building work, which meant a further drain on the RBK loan. Bernie McDermott offered a strategy for fundraising over the following year, which confidently anticipated smaller sums coming in as a result of the big investment from GMH. It was difficult to share his confidence – not least because of such interminable uncertainty – and tensions inevitably flared into the open. It was an unhappy situation.

The University remained positive and supportive throughout all these tortuous processes. In a demonstration of confidence and in addition to his chancellorship, Peter Hall was named Professor and so he became the first professor of my Drama Department. At the same time, the University created a new school, the School of Performance and Screen Studies, to which I was appointed the inaugural Head. One of our major postgraduate courses would be our new Master of Fine Arts in Classical Theatre Practice, which would be at the centre of the work of the Rose. Hall was in his element discussing the MFA and we spent many hours planning it during the week. Sundays were reserved for long telephone calls about the theatre's progress: Peter seemed to suffer bouts of pessimism and uncertainty on Sundays. In the Autumn, he perked up as Melvyn Bragg's Southbank Show filmed a two part programme, some of it made in the Rose, in recognition of Hall's fifty years in theatre.

The difficulties within the Trust and the uneasiness which had developed between the trustees and the executive was not resolved entirely when McDermott resigned, which he did in October. His one target strategy – pin down GMH and £3 million – showed little sign of being concluded successfully. So long as he had the support of Peter Hall I suppose he felt protected, but I can only assume he must have been frustrated too by his own inability to bring home any goods of note. But there were other problems: the Trust had been in existence for a decade and a half and the distance left to travel seemed so small yet frustratingly out of reach. Had the Trust handed over to an executive team and seen the conclusion quickly reached all would have been well. The trustees needed to leave things to the executive to get on with, but the funding impasse meant that both bodies were left very vulnerable. The differences and divisions became palpable: I well remember meeting with a member of the executive and one of the design team, the latter of whom was told that it was fine to speak with Frank here: 'he's one of us'. I was a little disconcerted at this sense of divisiveness, and certainly did not identify with particular camps. I was concerned to keep everyone moving forward towards the ultimate goal of achieving a fully fitted-out theatre. Peter was, perhaps inevitably, always the elephant at these times, whether in the room or out, and I fairly frequently tried to act as keeper. He could be very difficult, especially when there was stress and uncertainty and I saw it as my role to try and calm the waters, not always with success. It was, however, a time when the diplomacy of David Jacobs and good counsel of Bruce Macdonald were of importance in bringing stability and keeping the Trust and RBK working together.

When, in January 2006, GMH nominated three directors there was no sense that this would lead necessarily to a positive outcome and both RBK and KTT agreed to a deadline of the end of February to resolve all matters with regard to the new company. David Fletcher had already estimated that an opening delayed till September 2007 probably added somewhere around half a million pounds to the project's price to completion, taking into account operational costs, fees and inflation. In January the KTT Board asked the Executive to produce a contingency report.

David Fletcher, Sue Higginson and Peter Hall prepared this paper in February setting out their views on the way ahead, should the £3 million pledge from GMH not materialise. It made for pretty bleak reading. They felt that at the beginning of 2005 the project had had a real momentum, but this had largely evaporated during the year till now. We were all acutely aware that questions were being asked in public and that political difficulties were growing. For them, they were becoming increasingly uncomfortable – rightly – about the cost to the local taxpayer of keeping the executive team together. They examined what they saw as funding alternatives for the completion of the capital project and also at the current and deteriorating financial position. The available working capital came almost entirely from the RBK Loan Facility, with approximately £30,000 a year from the Friends and other small donations. Already nearly half of the second loan facility, intended to provide the necessary working capital to build the organisation through to the opening of the theatre, had been spent. Should more time be lost, further funds would be needed for the organisation and building phase. To restore confidence in the project, and to minimise the risk to the local taxpayer, they felt it was essential that any new funding initiative must be able to deliver in full within a few months. However, the various alternatives that they listed had little chance of success on such a timescale. Their conclusion was that if it was clear that GMH would not provide the funding the whole project should be mothballed, staff given notice, the office closed and public notice given.

At the beginning of March, there had been what was thought a productive meeting with Mr Auchi and GMH, with a proposal for investment in the form of a debenture. By late March a further four conditions which Mr Auchi was concerned about – unpaid distribution, forced transfer on default, failure of the theatre lease, and other 'reserved' matters – were apparently successfully negotiated away, although the debenture route now was seen not to provide the tax efficiency GMH wanted. However, the RBK executive, which was driving the negotiation, felt they could move forward on this agreement.

One interesting and quiet event occurred in March: Michael Boyd and others from the Royal Shakespeare Company made a visit to Kingston. They were in the process of completing the design for their new Stratford theatre. According to Peter, who had for so long trumpeted the great virtues of our Rose 'Lozenge', they were impressed and as a result were having second thoughts and were considering adapting the shape of their proposed new stage. Anyone who has been to Stratford since will know that they evidently had third thoughts too: the Stratford stage is a long tongue stretching into the auditorium, a larger version of the Swan and nothing at all like the Rose!

In early May, a negotiating process which had been engaged for over two years was brought to an abrupt halt: the difficulty apparently related to the question of what would happen in the event of default. It had been agreed previously by both parties that in the event of a default the innocent party would have the right to buy out the defaulting party. GMH now proposed, with regard to this eventuality, that the *defaulting* party be given the right to buy out the *innocent* party at a fair value plus 5%. Obviously, there was a risk that one party might *engineer* a default and thus get their hands on a valuable building and freehold. This was a significant departure from previous positions and obviously one which neither the Council nor the Trust could even contemplate. GMH would obviously have to return to their previously held position, but it quickly became obvious that this would not happen. The deal was off, but it had been a costly diversion!

One can only ask questions about motive and we will never know why we were held up for two years over a negotiation which reached a point which would evidently be unacceptable and which would, if suggested at the outset, have been dismissed without further consideration. Looking back, Chris Blackhurst, who was then City Editor of the *Evening Standard* and also a trustee, feels it was simply the irreconcilable situation of the demands of someone whose interests were in business and the need, on the other side, to protect a public asset. Blackhurst has also reflected on the fact that so much effort was put into chasing down one agreement with one particular individual, whilst not looking very much further. Fundraising time had been wasted.

The Royal Borough of Kingston now took a contentious but brave decision, which posterity should applaud them for. On Tuesday 20th June the RBK Executive allocated £3.4 million to underwrite the completion of the fit-out. Mr Auchi was told that the commercial requirements of GMH were evidently inconsistent with the Borough's obligation to secure and safeguard a public asset. The theatre would effectively be owned by RBK and Kingston University, as Kingston Theatre Limited Liability Partnership. Needless to say, there was a sense of relief at this outcome: it seemed so much more apposite than other prospects. The Leader of the Council, Derek Osbourne, would have to carry the proposal at a full Council meeting in August, which duly happened. On that evening, as the final part of the political jig-saw fell into place, I was sitting out under the night sky on Mount Parnassus in a campsite near the Shrine of Delphi, high above the Gulf of Corinth, when Sue Higginson sent a message: 'You have your theatre'. It was an auspicious moment and soon text messages came from all over the world in response to my elated missives.

A few months earlier Peter Hall had reflected on the character of our project: 'This is the next chapter in a peculiarly English story that I have been observing all my working life. Rose of Kingston was not brought into being as part of a national plan for the arts; it has not been backed by the Arts Council or funded by the Lottery. It is a purely local initiative bred of the enthusiasm of riverside residents and the vision of the local authority'. Meanwhile, eyes were turning towards Kingston again. Commenting on Peter Hall's current work, Charles Spencer wrote in *The Daily Telegraph* in July: 'You have to take your hat off to Peter Hall. At 75 his theatrical energy shows no sign of flagging as his annual summer season at Bath kicks off with three plays on the subject of sex and sexual frustration ... Shakespeare's *Measure for Measure*, Strindberg's *Miss Julie*, and Alan Bennett's farce *Habeas Corpus*. Having got that load off his mind, as it were, Hall's company then offers two of the key dramatic works of the 20th century, Beckett's *Waiting for Godot*, and a 50th anniversary staging of Osborne's *Look Back in Anger*. It's a characteristically rich and ambitious season that makes one long for the day when Hall is safely established in his new Rose Theatre in Kingston. This is a director enjoying a glorious Indian summer'. If Hall's Indian summer did not endure in Kingston, his very presence played its part in the drama.

Had the Rose cost Kingston more than originally thought, when the idea was that we would have an arts centre or a theatre? Recalling that in 1989 the Royal Borough of Kingston pledged £4 million to the theatre project and anticipated some annual revenue funding need of £300,000, a calculation of this value in 2006, taking into account inflation during the intervening years, suggests that the capital figure, to maintain its value, would be £7.2 million. This is probably marginally more than RBK eventually had in the end to commit, taking into account both capital sums and loan agreements. It is a pity that the theatre has been a political football, especially during the difficult years leading up to the final opening. It was, after all, a Tory administration, with all party support, which oversaw the initial allocation of £4 million in the budget in 1989 (which the Tory councillor and KTT director Jim Daly famously referred to years later as 'a line in the capital budget which was stolen'); it was a Liberal Democrat administration under John Tilley which 'stole' that line and announced that the National Lottery could take care of funding; it was a Liberal Democrat administration which stepped in to fund the fit-out of the theatre and a Tory opposition group which attacked this. Had they all maintained their original stance we'd have had the theatre earlier, but probably not the very special theatre that we now have.

As though in anticipation of this outcome, long-serving trustee Mary Reid had become Mayor of Kingston in May 2006 and the Kingston Readers' Festival had yet another successful year under the super-charged leadership of Sandy Williams. Each of them epitomised public-spirited Kingstonians who had contributed so much to what was now Kingston's own theatre.

16
Beginnings and Endings

By the end of July 2006 building activity inside the theatre was underway and with the knowledge that the fit-out would be completed by late Autumn the following year. A new Development Group was looking for both money towards the capital funding which RBK had underwritten and at the need for revenue funding, both to establish and to sustain an artistic programme. New fundraisers were being sought and the Friends, whose numbers had understandably dwindled to fewer than 1000 during the hiatus, were now working to re-engage lapsed members. The Friends were quickly rejuvenated with a theatre floor-signing event, to which over 500 came.

The mood of optimism was blunted for me when Peter Hall quietly told some of us that he would not be able to carry the burden of being artistic director beyond the opening of the theatre. It was not entirely surprising: he had been seventy-two years old when we appointed him and the subsequent years of uncertainty had been a drain. By the time the theatre opened he would be nearly eighty and facing some arduous time both establishing the work and also seeing the training programme start successfully. We persuaded him that no announcement about this should be made until we had found a successor. In the first instance, David Jacobs asked Peter and me to find a replacement we might recommend to the board.

Many names were soon a part of our conversation, most of whom Hall would be able to speak to quite easily. Trevor Nunn, we knew, was very taken with the Rose, but might well not want a job running a building again – as it was to prove. Edward Hall would crop up in conversation often: he had already experience behind him both running the Watermill Theatre, Newbury and also as the founding director of Propeller, a company he committed to vibrant (all male) productions of Shakespeare. The father had evidently discussed things with the son: David Fletcher was a little taken aback when Edward Hall arrived in Kingston one day and asked to 'see the books'. Jude Kelly suggested Tom Morris, who was currently doing great work at the National. Marianne Elliott, whose production at the National Theatre of Ibsen's *Pillars of the Community* had very recently won the *Evening Standard Best Director* award, was high on our list, although apparently she had expressed her preference for working in a theatre with other associate directors attached. Her subsequent brilliant career has been characterised by quality collaborations.

In the first instance, however, Hall suggested Thea Sharrock. Sharrock was one of the exciting young British directors at work: she had become artistic director at the Southwark Playhouse at the age of twenty-four and now, still in her twenties, was in charge at the Gate. For the Peter Hall Company, she had had success with Pinter, Rattigan, Coward and Moliere, but no Shakespeare. I went straight up to the Gate to see her production of Ionesco's *The Chairs* and was impressed. She was well aware that we were very interested in her coming to Kingston: I had written to her and one Friday morning in late November I spoke at length to her on the telephone; that evening I received a message from Peter saying: 'I've had a good meeting with Thea, though she's not sure she feels she can commit. She wants time to consider … I've asked her to let us know as soon as possible. She did tell me that you'd made contact – so let's keep our fingers crossed'.

It was quite reasonable that we should wait for Sharrock to weigh up all of the possibilities before deciding finally. She wrote to Peter in January and it was, he said, clear that she wanted to take up the job of Artistic Director, but equally she had genuine worries. As a young professional mother, she relied on her North London family. Finally, sadly, she decided against: I suspect that she would have been outstanding, but it was not to be. Kingston's loss was the gain of many from the West End and Broadway audiences for her production of *Equus* (the stage debut of Daniel Radcliffe) and to the worldwide viewers of her fabulous TV/Film production of *Henry V* with Tom Hiddleston in *The Hollow Crown* series.

And so we had to re-focus our search. In early February 2007 I wrote to Greg Doran. I admired Doran's work, perhaps at that time for one main reason, although so much else has happened since: he was the mastermind behind the RSC's 2002 Swan season of Jacobean and Elizabethan plays. With a number of different directors involved, the plays transferred to the Gielgud from December 2002 to March 2003, which coincided with our Season in the Shell. The plays were: *The Malcontent* by John Webster & John Marston; *The Roman Actor* by Philip Massinger; *Edward III* by Shakespeare; *Eastward Ho!* by George Chapman, Ben Jonson & John Marston; and *The Island Princess* by John Fletcher which Doran himself directed. What a repertoire! Doran's partner Antony Sher led the company and he was dazzling in *The Roman Actor* as the decadent Emperor Domitian. This play, a dark tragi-comedy, is a debate about the legitimacy of theatre. It gave Sher, as a *Guardian* review said, 'a chance to add Domitian to his repertoire of hypnotic villains ... In a play packed with theatrical metaphors, he suggests even dictators are actors.' *The Roman Actor* was directed by Sean Holmes, another name on our long list.

Thelma Holt had produced the London 2003 season having inveigled, she suggested herself, much of the capital needed from Duncan Kenwright. In a delightfully brazen interview with Fiona Maddocks in the *Evening Standard*, she recalled a visit to Stratford the year before: 'Greg invited me up to see [the plays]. "You must come, Thelma. We so want to see you". I knew exactly what he wanted. His fairy godmother blessed him with so much damn charm. We sat in his garden. He gave me tuna sandwiches. He knows I like tuna. They're such tarts, these directors'. And what if someone from the RSC other than Doran had asked her? 'I'd have told them, "Bugger off". But it was too late. I'd seen the plays. The audience was having such a ball. I was sunk'. Holt made one condition: she 'insisted that all 28 performers have 'flu injections, because understudies cannot be afforded'.

Writing about the success of the season at the Swan, Doran showed how he has a natural capacity for knowing the moment: 'I suspect they have struck such a chord because the period in which they were written has many parallels with our own age. It was an age of anxiety and disillusion, of uncertainty and insecurity. Of pessimism and cynicism, of changing morality and declining values; consequently, it was also a time in which irony, satire and dark comedy flourished. And the theatre flourished too ...'

On one of my Gielgud visits to the productions back in 2003 I had sought out Doran to tell him about the Rose and he called Thelma Holt over. They were evidently enjoying their collaboration enormously. It was around the time that we were finalising Peter Hall's appointment to Kingston and when Michael Boyd, rather than Doran, was taking over the RSC from Adrian Noble. I said to him that maybe at some time in the future we could lure him to Kingston. 'Lovely', he said, winking to Holt, 'and you could come too, Thelma, but if Peter's there I don't think there'll be enough room for us!' They laughed. Thelma Holt had done time with the Peter Hall Company.

Looking back to 2003, I thought that Greg Doran had given the RSC as good a calling card for the top job as anyone might. In a *Guardian* interview in 2002, when he was tipped to become the next Artistic Director at Stratford, he had said, 'My area is with classical work, which I think we do need to celebrate on the larger stage, training younger directors to work with big spaces: opportunities like that are getting fewer. There is a fashionable trend toward more intimate spaces, which is valid, but classical work requires specific disciplines and crafts'. The RSC overlooked him and appointed Michael Boyd, who proved enormously successful. Could we capitalise? Peter Hall was reticent: he thought Doran a good director, but was 'too much of the showman'. I disagreed and Doran's remark above, along with his record, seemed to me admirably to qualify him for a role which, in addition to creating great productions, would have seen him work with a new generation through the university course.

When Thea Sharrock finally declined in February we invited Doran to come to Kingston. Peter and I showed him around the theatre, where Rosie Hoare and her team were well underway towards completing the fit-out, although it was still a hard-hat space. I think that Doran was interested, but the uncertainty around funding into the future was obviously a major obstacle. When he did telephone a few days later, he was very candid both about what he saw, which he admired, but also about his position at the RSC. He had evidently been temporarily upset that he had not been given the artistic directorship, but said that Michael Boyd had been extremely generous to him, giving him both control of the Swan and a free hand on choice of productions with the company. It was a kind of power without responsibility: he said he thought he had perhaps the best job in British theatre, so it would be foolhardy to throw it over. Anyone looking at Doran's career would have to agree: just over five years later he was rightly made Artistic Director at Stratford, following on the brilliant resuscitation of the company under Boyd and he took it from strength to strength – and, I think, has given the lie to Hall's assessment of him. My only quibble with both Boyd and Doran, for I am sure the latter must have been involved, is over the design of the new stage in the main house at Stratford. But more of that anon.

So Greg Doran did not come to Kingston either, but Thelma Holt – in a little twist of fate – did two years later, when she succeeded me, amongst others, as a director of the Kingston Theatre Trust.

We were in a quandary and Hall was beginning to fret. We had agreed that there would be no announcement about his retirement until we had found a replacement. Not only were the members of the Trust aware of the situation, but a number of Councillors and therefore some RBK officers were too: there was a concern about a leak. So we now needed to make progress. Whoever replaced him, Peter would stay on as Director Emeritus which would include at least one or two productions a year. We also had an opening programme to plan and, of course, the on-going headache of revenue funding. Peter felt that we should be casting the net more widely and had heard that Stephen Unwin was shortly to leave English Touring Theatre. When Stephen telephoned me one Sunday evening a few weeks later, he said that he was very interested in the Kingston job. I guessed that Peter had prompted him.

If Stephen Unwin became Artistic Director a little by default he was, nevertheless, brave in throwing in his lot with a project which might not survive long into the opening. Sue Higginson had announced her resignation just before Peter Hall, having been seriously ill during the previous year. Most fortunately, David Fletcher was on hand to step up and for the next few years was a calming and fiscally reassuring presence.

Unwin had already had an eclectic career as a director, writer and teacher. He had founded English Touring Theatre in 1993 and ten years later, in 2003, shared the Sam Wanamaker award with Barrie Rutter, who had himself that very year played such an important role in helping the Rose establish itself. Unwin had been involved with the National Theatre Studio in Sue Higginson's time and also with drama schools and universities in Britain and the USA. One of the first things he said to me was that he was attracted by the prospects of the teaching programme created by Peter Hall in association with the university. He spent much of the eighties as an associate director at Edinburgh's Traverse Theatre, directing formidable actors there, such as Alan Cumming, Kathryn Hunter and Simon Russell Beale. When he founded ETT in 1993 he continued to attract good actors, notably when Timothy and Samuel West played father and son in *Henry 1V Pts 1&2* at the Old Vic. Both Tim West (for *King Lear*) and Diana Quick (for *Ghosts*) won TMA (Theatrical Management Association, now UK Theatre) awards in his productions. Alexandra Gilbreath won the 1996 Ian Charleson award for *Hedda Gabler*, which also won for Unwin the TMA award for Best Touring Production.

Unwin must have realised pretty quickly that he was not stepping into a comfortable role. When Hall had announced the previous Autumn that he wanted to step down, it was suggested that he be Artistic Director Emeritus in order to keep the Rose moving forward and to effect a smooth transfer. The intervening months were characterised by the difficulties in finding a replacement and then complicated by the negotiations over what Hall's reduced salary and obligations would be. His salary as Artistic Director had always been made up of funds provided by KTT combined with a contribution from Kingston University. For years, Hall had spoken with such enthusiasm of his plans to engage the theatre and the university in an innovative project, but now argued that his Emeritus role, with a salary attached, should not include any involvement with the university. I was somewhat taken aback. He wrote to Gail Cunningham and me in June 2007 and was blunt: 'First, please understand how much I have valued our working relationship. Nonetheless, I really cannot see what would be gained by us meeting about the MFA Course when fundamental issues within the whole Rose project remain unresolved ... As you are both aware, my interest has, from day one, been purely to create a unique environment for young theatre students. Within this, they would have not only the highest quality academic tuition, but from the outset be integrated into the professional theatre environment. No one else in the UK is offering this – but, sadly, we now can't achieve it either'. For Hall, it seemed, the battle was probably over and he wanted to place himself at arms length from a part of the project to which he had seemed so bound during the previous four years.

Meanwhile, the Rose itself was struggling for survival yet again. An insolvency consultant was brought in to guide KTT through important decision-making. The completed theatre would be handed over to the Trust in December and the opening season should begin in January 2008. We could open the theatre in January 2008 with two productions if we had £600,000 in place. To complete the opening season up until July would need a further £1.1 million. The hope was to open the season with two productions, one of which would be *The Tempest*, directed by Hall. These would be joint Bath Festival and English Touring Theatre productions. KTT would be the presenter unless it could raise sponsorship and so be a co-producer.

David Fletcher produced a budget, which remained a consistent and surprisingly accurate guide throughout the period, given the shifting tides. What's more, he acted as the pilot through these difficult waters. Fletcher's careful, unflappable and balanced approach in the most difficult of situations was a critical factor in seeing the theatre through to its successful opening seasons.

To help maintain the season, we could call on Northern Broadsides who had already established a following from 2003. I offered a production of *The Ragged Child* for a week, which would come with no production costs to the theatre. I was confident that a revival would be a success. The writing team of David Nield (composer and a Rose trustee), Jeremy James Taylor and me (Book and Lyrics) would waive our performing rights and directorial fees and it would be a Kingston University production and so 'free at the point of delivery' to the Rose.

Fundraising slowly improved. Iain More Associates had been engaged, and More himself proved to be flexible and imaginative to a degree. By the middle of the year £124,000 had been raised and a further potential £180,000 identified towards the required budget. For the first time, Wahid Samedy made an appearance: Barry O'Mahony encouraged the chairman of CNM Estates, which was involved in a number of local building developments, to become involved and Samedy offered to underwrite the season with £400,000. Here was a businessman who quickly and generously responded in the interests of the arts. This enabled David Fletcher to present a budget in early September, but owing to a shortfall still of some £100,000 he had to recommend that we reject it. It was yet another watershed moment. Three trustees, Barry O'Mahony, Gail Cunningham and Roger Chown generously and remarkably responded and were able to assure a total of £45,000, while Iain More was confident enough to guarantee £55,000 from promised donations. Fletcher was able to change his recommendation and the Board ratified it: the Rose would open.

Hall said he was now unable to cast the role of Prospero in *The Tempest*, but offered *Uncle Vanya*, which both ETT and Bath were happy with. I thought it was a good choice because not obvious: the expectation might have been for, if not Shakespeare, a play from the original sixteenth century Rose repertoire or another Elizabethan or Jacobean play. We knew the Rose worked well for the latter, having already seen productions of *Henry V*, *A Woman Killed with Kindness* and *As You Like It* during the 'Shell' years. Nearly five years after Barrie Rutter stepped onto the stage and uttered:

O for a Muse of fire, that would ascend
The brightest heaven of invention,
A kingdom for a stage, princes to act
And monarchs to behold the swelling scene ...

we would open the Rose to the quiet rhythms of Chekhov, offering tea and vodka and musing on wasted years and aspirations for a better future.

17
The Star of this opening season ...

David Jacobs announced in November 2007 that he would step down as Chairman of Kingston Theatre Trust at the end of the following January, after the official opening. He would, thus, have seen in the opening production in the theatre which, during nearly twenty years, he had fought for. He was already over eighty, but had been undaunted by set backs and strife. Several years later, when he died, I wrote my own note of gratitude to David and it appeared in *The Guardian*:

> David Jacobs' versatility and spirit were qualities invaluable in making an impact in the arts beyond the world of radio and television broadcasting. In 1989 he became the first Chairman of the Kingston Theatre Trust, a role he fulfilled with wit, dogged determination and no small amount of ingenuity as we strove for nearly twenty years to build 'the first theatre of the twenty first century'. In January 2008, the Rose Theatre, Kingston opened with Peter Hall's production of *Uncle Vanya*. The suggestion years before that Kingston's theatre should be modelled on one built in 1587, during the reign of Queen Elizabeth 1, momentarily took David aback: he had envisaged a stage with a proscenium arch and plush seats. Within two minutes he had warmed to the idea and then his imagination became gripped. During his two decades leading the theatre's board there were difficult times,

> not least financially, but David's optimism and refusal to be
> thwarted were crucial in keeping the project afloat. There can
> have been few more warming sights than to see his broad smile
> which – until very recently – would light up every opening night.
> The Rose is a unique memorial to Jacobs' commitment to the arts
> in general.

David Jacobs had become a very good and generous friend, particularly to me and Robin Hutchinson. For several years past David's friend Stuart, a neighbouring Sussex farmer of his and his wife Lesley, would act as a chauffeur driving him to Broadcasting House, where he would record *The David Jacobs Collection* for Radio 2, before coming on to Kingston for our meetings. He would insist on giving me a lift home afterwards, so that at least for a short part of the way to Sussex he and Stuart would have someone to mediate in their gentle and amused banter. We would stop at the City Arms just south of Kingston where Stuart would have half a pint, I would have a pint and David would have 'a large whisky, my dear'. He would take a plastic cup out of his pocket and divide his whisky, the second part being 'carry-out' for the journey back to Sussex.

One evening, the Summer before the theatre opening, we had been in a particularly gruelling meeting and David stayed for a drink afterwards in the Druid's Head with Robin Hutchinson and me. He and Robin alleviated the feeling of frustration and despondency, sitting side by side and breaking into song with popular tunes from past times of strife – 'It's a long way to Tipperary ...' and 'You are my sunshine ...' and 'Pack up your troubles ...' – with an air of light-hearted satire.

Hutchinson himself became acting Chairman of the Board, whilst a successor was sought and he found himself overseeing what was a difficult period of six months. Anthony Simonds-Gooding was eventually recruited and he came with the promising tag of being the ad-man who had signed off on Heineken being the drink which can 'refresh the parts other beers cannot reach'. This engaging Irishman, with his roots in County Kerry, was charged by Kingston Council and the University with beginning a reformation of the Trust and within a year many of us had stepped aside.

The December and January leading up to the Opening Night of the Rose was an odd time for me as I became, for the first time in my life, rather seriously ill and found myself in hospital for much of the time, so missing some of the excitement! I was suffering from acute pancreatitis and the medics were concerned that it might be a sign of something rather worse. As Wednesday 16th January – Opening Night – approached, I mentioned to a doctor that I had a rather important engagement on that day. She smiled and said that she was very sorry, but that was one event that I would have to miss. Surely, said Roger Chown, they'll let you out for a few hours, attached though I was to drips and catheters. Fortunately, amongst the team of doctors were two supporters of the Rose and, after some deliberation, they agreed that I could be sprung, but – though with little resemblance to Cinderella – I'd have to be back on my way to the ward as soon as the show came down. Roger kindly forewent some of the festivities and acted as my escort and ensured that the champagne glass I was given had but one bubble in the bottom. As far as I was concerned, it was a glass more than half full.

It was an extraordinary night. On arrival, one of the first faces I saw was David Fletcher's, who had a look of boyish delight, even though he had been taxed by a great gouge in the beautiful wooden flooring, made as the temporary bar was being dragged into position at the last minute. Robin Hutchinson and I hugged silently, then he muttered something about a dream. Rosie Hoare had not quite thrown off the burden of responsibility she had shouldered so brilliantly and uncomplainingly for five years past, but she had thrown off her hard hat. And there were the Friends, many already in the guise of ushers and programme sellers, perhaps the most significant force of people to bring this moment about.

Peter Hall had brought together a fine cast to play Chekhov's great tragi-comedy of wished-for-fulfilment, desperate sadness and disillusionment. Stephen Mulrine's new and colloquial translation of *Uncle Vanya* should be suited ideally to a space that had already captured attention for its ability to stage the intimate. Alison Chitty had stayed on beyond her design of the theatre fit-out to demonstrate why she is one of the world's great stage designers: her design was of wooden floors and grey furniture, both apt and mirroring her internal realisation of the Rose itself.

As the lights went down there was a spontaneous burst of applause, followed by a long and loud vocal sound, a sort of deep and resonating cheer. I felt my eyes welling. The sound was for the theatre, for the years of waiting and born of the relief that it was now here. Sean Duggan, editor of the *Surrey Comet*, recalled that sound some days later: 'It seemed to come from everywhere and nowhere at the same time – as if the building itself was celebrating its final awakening into life. It sent a shiver down my spine'.

The national press would be on hand, but it was the local *Surrey Comet*, at last becoming a firm supporter, which led the acclaim on the opening: 'Today marks the start of a new era in the life of Kingston when the Rose Theatre finally opens its doors', wrote the *Comet's* chief reporter, Alita Howe. 'Many people thought it would never happen, but despite all the obstacles, it has and the £11 million Rose is a unique world-class theatre'. Robin Hutchinson was quoted as being 'still in a sense of disbelief' at the realisation of a dream. I, apparently, said I was 'chuffed to bits' and praised 'the powerful and influential triumvirate of Kingstonians themselves, the Royal Borough of Kingston and the University' which had made it a reality. David Jacobs was 'overwhelmed with disbelief – it's all too wonderful for words'!

Yet again, the national critics followed large audiences to Kingston for the Press Night on 25th January. Paul Taylor in *The Independent*, continued his bombs falling on theatrical bigwigs comment with: 'These luminaries had descended in droves on [Hall's] beautifully acted production, because it inaugurates a brand new theatre, the Rose of Kingston'. The acting was excellent, of course: Ronald Pickup's Serebryakov showed 'the selfishness of old age rather than mere selfishness' (*Curtain Up*); Michelle Dockery 'is pitch-perfect as the beautiful Yelena' (*The Daily Telegraph*); 'I've never seen Nicholas Le Provost better ... he avoids the usual passivity and suggests a Vanya who is simmering and bubbling with resentment, boiling with thwarted desire ...' (*The Times*); 'In an evening of excellent characterisations, Neil Pearson's Astrov is foremost' (*The Financial Times*); no one escaped a good notice!

However, just as five years previously, it was the theatre which won the critics' awards. Nick Curtis in *The Evening Standard* pronounced it, 'the best modern theatre I know'. It was pleasing to see how well the theatre worked for Chekhov: 'all aspects, including the Rose space itself', wrote Ian Shuttleworth in *The Financial Times*, 'combine so that we feel we are not so much being offered a window on to these people's thoughts and feelings as witnessing them from within the room'. Benedict Nightingale wrote of 'an elegant reworking of an Elizabethan original ... but, boy, it looks and feels good ...' (*The Times*). And Lizzie Loveridge helped encourage audiences out of London and only just stopped short of handing out maps and train timetables with: 'The star of this opening season is the new theatre, the Rose of Kingston upon Thames, just to the south west of London and half an hour on a train from Waterloo' (*Curtain Up*).

I was especially taken with the apparent ease with which actors were able to address the audience. Years before, Barrie Rutter and Conrad Nelson in *Henry V* and actors in Hall's *As You Like It* company had shown how effectively set piece speeches, soliloquies and asides worked in the Rose. Chekhov, so often associated with naturalism and notions of 'the fourth wall removed', now sounded crisp and conversational as actors spoke to the audience as if to other characters in the same room: they were confidential and felt natural. Nicholas Le Provost, as Vanya, was especially comfortable in his conversations with the audience. The space suited the play, and so at an early stage the Rose revealed its versatility. Maev Kennedy wrote that 'when Loo Brealey spoke Sonia's desolating last words in *Uncle Vanya*, it was as though she was murmuring into every ear in the audience' (*The Guardian*).

Susannah Clapp, for *The Observer*, had had more time for reflection and touched on some wider truths and contexts, but found herself giving the last word neither to herself nor a fellow critic, but to a loyal Kingstonian giving of their time:

> The real heroine of the evening, though, is the Rose itself ... it's an unpretentiously excellent space ... that allows closeness as well as airiness. Some audience members sit (for £7) on cushions directly in front of the stage, where they look as though they're being told a story by the fireside. The bad news is that, with no core funding, there isn't yet enough money to create a resident

company, or to develop Hall's plan for a working relationship with Kingston University, which would allow students to train in the theatre as actors, directors and designers. The Rose – which has bloomed in the weeks when so many stages were under attack from Arts Council cuts – deserves better. 'This is very nice', a critical voice announced behind me. Beside him, an usher was quick to put him right: 'It's not nice, it's fabulous'.

Taken in all, it was an auspicious opening to a first full season in the Rose. I was delighted that our production of *The Ragged Child* drew large audiences, as did the return of Northern Broadsides with *Romeo and Juliet*. For *The Ragged Child* we put together an artistic team, all donating their work, of experienced National Youth Music Theatre practitioners, including long-term collaborators of mine: besides Jeremy James Taylor and David Nield, there was Joanna Billington , John Pearson and Christopher Richardson. Our lighting designer was another NYMT luminary and fellow Rose trustee, Richard House, who had done so much to help the Rose into being. We revived the production which had been something of a flagship of the NYMT for the past two decades. It had brought players like Jude Law and Jonny Lee Miller, Rebecca Lock and Charles Edwards, Stephen Graham and Jamie Parker, Sarah Lawn and the future director Jo Davies to the public eye for the first time. This present company was drawn from Kingston University Drama students and from local schools and during the performance week the average audience attendance was 580, contributing just short of £50,000 in box office. I had directed productions of this ballad opera in many theatres: in Norway at the Bergen Festival, in Toronto and New York; at Sadler's Wells, at the Riverside Studios for the BBC and at Glyndebourne, on the Edinburgh International Festival and in regional theatres around the country. It is a play which dramatises in words and music the epic struggle for survival of Joe and Annie Cooper, two of thirty thousand destitute children in London in 1849, a century and a half before. The action moves from the lodging houses of London and the ragged schools (encouraged by the reforming Earl of Shaftesbury) to Australia, either on convict or emigration ships. The set, designed by

Christopher Richardson, was simply a large open cart, which could swing through 360 degrees and which could carry nearly all of the cast of over thirty in dramatic set pieces and great tableaux. The whole company was on stage throughout, when not involved in the action sitting on benches in an open semi-circle around the world of the play. Critical comments in years gone by had spoken of epic moments and of heart-searing and tragic scenes, notably when Joe loses his sister Annie, succumbing to the plague of cholera. Nowhere did our staging work so well as it did at the Rose in 2008.

With the oft-mentioned monetary caveats ringing in his ears, Stephen Unwin was undergoing a baptism by fire. His appointment as successor to Peter Hall was announced formally on 21ˢᵗ January, just after *Uncle Vanya* opened. His first task was to try to develop the Rose's identity with a strategic plan. He came up with an idea initially for a National Centre for the Spoken Word, with revenue potential and a substantial education programme at its heart. Later the narrative was refined: the Rose was a theatre which would put an *emphasis* on the spoken word. He was also trying to create the second season in the knowledge that this would, one way or another, establish the artistic identity.

It was inevitably going to be difficult to open a theatre and sustain performance work without some substantial working capital and without any grant funding. During a difficult Summer and early Autumn, Trust meetings had been held with financial and legal advice to hand to ensure that unsustainable commitments were not made. We were frequently faced with the decision either to move forward tentatively, or to mothball the theatre and wait for funding, a course none of us wanted to take. There was also need for 'letters of comfort' from stakeholders.

There had been some generous support: the Garfield Weston Foundation, not for the first time, helped; Roger Chown spirited very good sums from local businesses, including £50,000 from the restaurant Frère Jacques. Wahid Samedy of CNM Estates then came to help again offering to provide some underwriting which eventually enabled planning of the Autumn season. Arts Council England at last gave some support in the form of a one-off £48,000 grant. Various artists gave free performances, too: my daughter, the singer-songwriter Martha Tilston, contributed a

sell-out evening of *Martha Tilston and Friends* which included Maggie
Boyle playing alongside Mick Sands, who himself had composed the music
for Hall's opening production of *Uncle Vanya*.

Unwin's Spoken Word idea gave some sort of a logic in choosing *Loves
Labours Lost* as the first Rose production, but it was Peter Hall's choice
and he would direct it. There would be a programme including 'Language
of Love' workshops and a poetry competition. The season would be filled
out with other Peter Hall Company productions from its Theatre Royal
Bath summer season, with Unwin directing the Peter Nichols play *Born in
the Gardens*, starring Stephanie Cole while Hall himself directed *A Doll's
House* and *The Portrait of a Lady* adapted from the Henry James novel for
the stage by Hall's wife, Nicki Frei, and starring strong casts including
Jean Marsh, Finbar Lynch alongside Catherine McCormack and Niamh
Cusack. For this latter pair it would prove a prelude to their wonderful
return to the Rose nearly a decade later in *My Brilliant Friend*.

I was not the only one a little nervous about *Loves Labours Lost*.
Stephen Unwin tried to dissuade him, but Hall was determined: that's
what he was offering. Moth's mocking comment in the play to Costard
about Don Armado and Holofernes that, 'They have been at a great feast
of languages, and stol'n the scraps', has often been used to characterise
the play itself: a great feast of language. In retrospect, and despite some
positive critical notices, it was not a good choice for a number of reasons.
It is *not* a particularly popular play, despite some notable productions such
as Peter Brook's astonishing debut over sixty years before. Perhaps the
best reason for not doing it at this particular moment was that two weeks
earlier the RSC had opened a production with David Tennant, himself
fresh from rave notices as Hamlet, playing Berowne. The RSC production
was directed by Greg Doran and was both critically acclaimed and popular,
though possibly demonstrated some of the characteristics of Doran which
Hall had reservations about – his showmanship, which others see as a
part of his attractive versatility. Mark Espiner in *The Guardian* wrote that
the RSC version 'seeks to distract us from the knotty complexity of the
words', while Michael Billington wrote of the Rose production in the same
paper that Hall 'confronts and delights in the play's verbal games'. Both
were staged in Elizabethan costume and each drew attention to the spaces

they were played in, in Stratford the temporary but attractive Courtyard. I wonder still whether Peter Hall was purposefully challenging the young upstart Doran, who had turned Kingston down, though as yet not leading the company Hall had himself founded nearly fifty years before. The RSC programme was known long before the Rose was able to make a commitment. A comparison of the two productions was inevitable which Hall would have anticipated. Charles Spencer – so often eagerly antic-ipating Hall's tenure at the Rose – wrote of his 'doctrinaire approach' and said, 'In Stratford, the director Gregory Doran treated it as a romp, with Tennant buttonholing the audience like a stand-up comic as the witty and irreverent courtier Berowne. In contrast, Hall takes matters far more seriously. He focuses single-mindedly on the language, with the supporting cast often standing mutely round the edge of the stage as the linguistic fireworks explode ' (*The Daily Telegraph*). Even a reviewer who assertively preferred Hall's version inadvertently suggested that this was not the play to show off Shakespeare in the completed Rose and as the first Rose Production. It was Peter Kirwan, a Warwick University scholar, in *Shakespeare Revue*:

> Hall's production was a world away from Doran's, particularly in its relative sobriety. A completely bare stage (save for some drapes lowered for the final pageant) focused all attention on the actors, dressed in beautifully individual Renaissance costume. Hall's measured approach eschewed silliness for silliness' sake, playing the text straight and placing entire faith in the words to draw laughs, where Doran's production seemed scared of the text and relied entirely on added business. One unfortunate effect of [Hall's] approach was to render the play rather dull, and this was felt most severely in the four male courtiers … This production perhaps didn't offer much for a casual audience, demanding a great deal in terms of listening, but was academically fascinating for the clarity with which it presented obscure verbal tics and jokes in an accessible and genuinely entertaining way.

If ever there was a time to please the groundlings and casual audiences – not necessarily with inexplicable dumb shows and noise – it was now. More scholarly Hall may have been, but the press notices were mixed and the box office was, unsurprisingly, disappointing.

Crucially, however, we had sustained a programme of work more or less continuously through the first year since opening. There was Unwin's production of *A Christmas Carol* to look forward to and it proved to be excellent. He was to demonstrate in this production a sure feel of how the playing space worked, helped especially by Simon Higlett's design. However, before all that we were back into a financial crisis. It was a very substantial and generous donation from Susie Sainsbury which allowed David Fletcher to negotiate further matched funding and which secured the future to the end of the year and into 2009. Fletcher's cool head and the confidence which others had in him came to the aid of the Rose yet again.

The relief of this news was reinforced by even better: joint action by both RBK and Kingston University gave the Rose stability for the first time in the form of a *New Deal* which offered the theatre comparative freedom to get on with its business at last. The joint commitment meant revenue funding of £800,000 a year.

18
A Decade in the limelight

In the years following that jubilant January night in 2008 the Rose has played a remarkable and varied role in the life of Kingston: the town is richer, culturally and economically; it has a renewed confidence; it is a better place to be both by day and by night; it is more outward-looking and it no longer falls back on tired Victorian notions about what it is. To these changes the Rose has contributed in large measure. The Rose has become a major regional theatre and is known nationally and internationally. That is not to say that it has fully realised its potential: a distinctive theatre – and the Rose is in many ways unique – needs to be able to stage a full programme of its own work, it needs to test itself, it needs to be innovative, it needs consistently to attract artists of the highest calibre, invention and imagination, it needs to draw in people of all ages, both as audience, but also as active participants.

Peter Hall's dream, along with my best efforts and those of Professors Brian Brivati, Colin Chambers and Ian Brown at the University, to create a teaching theatre of a unique nature which would feed into and draw from the artistic programme, have come to far less than we had ambitions for. Perhaps it was unrealistic even in 2003 to think that Hall, at the age of seventy three, would be able to commit his energies to a significant teaching programme at the same time as launching a new theatre with a year-long repertory programme. By 2008, when we opened, it was even less so and, despite his assertion that it was a problem of funding, Hall was by then tiring and nearly eighty. Money (or rather, the lack of it) and the passage of time struck wounding blows. The fact is that, while the idea is still alive, there is little prospect of realising it in the near future, without some startling philanthropic intervention allied to some public subsidy in keeping with the quality of work attempted and achieved. Also, in the intervening years Kingston University has veered away from the time when the Vice Chancellor was able to describe my Drama Department as 'a flagship of the University'.

Stephen Unwin was artistic director for six years. During that time he gave some master-classes to postgraduate students who were in turn included, peripherally, in productions such as *Miss Julie* (2009), *As You Like It* (2011), *The Lady from the Sea* (2012) and *The Vortex* (2013). Hall also gave some master-classes and included students in his renowned *A Midsummer Night's Dream* (2010). They were certainly valuable experiences for the students and offered some justification for specific university funding towards Rose Theatre productions, but they were not of the substantial and integrated nature which Hall and I had envisaged and which we had originally developed into our validated MFA course.

During his time at the Rose, Unwin directed some notably effective productions, always in the face of financial difficulties. As he said himself, 'The most important thing we do is present our own work'. *Miss Julie*, *Hay Fever* and *The Lady from the Sea* were amongst his best productions, whilst *The Winslow Boy* and *The Vortex* also received good critical notices. Perhaps surprising, given the special nature of the Rose, was the concentration of plays in his repertoire from the late nineteenth century and first half of the twentieth century. *Miss Julie* and *The Lady from the Sea* were first performed in 1889. Noel Coward's *The Vortex* and *Hay Fever* were from 1924 and 1925 respectively. Rattigan's *The Winslow Boy* (about an incident in 1908) and *The Browning Version*, from 1946 and 1948, were given Rose productions all in the same year, 2009. In 2011 Unwin directed both *The Importance of Being Earnest*, Oscar Wilde's enduring and brilliant satire from 1895, in repertory with Harley Granville Barker's 1916 play *Farewell to the Theatre*, which received its world premiere in this Rose production. There was certainly something apposite in that the heroine, Dorothy – played beautifully by Jane Asher – has wearied of the struggle to win financial sponsorship for her theatre. Unwin had inherited similar difficulties from Peter Hall and had battled on for three years, albeit supported by the ingenuity and patience of David Fletcher. Following the renewal of his contract for a further three years, in 2012, he directed Pinero's 1893 play *The Second Mrs Tanqueray*.

What is a little mystifying is that in a theatre crying out to be used to explore the rich repertoire of Elizabethan and Jacobean drama, Unwin chose not to draw from this golden age for his productions, an age which had inspired the building of this theatre in the first place. Only *As You Like It* in 2011 deviated from this, an odd choice in any case as Peter Hall had already directed his admired production 'In the Raw' in 2004. It was not as though Unwin did not have the experience, having directed previously about a dozen Shakespeare productions elsewhere, as well as *A Yorkshire Tragedy*, *The Changeling*, and from a little later Moliere's *Don Juan* and Farquhar's *The Beaux Stratagem*. He was eminently qualified to offer a Restoration classic or de Molina's *Don Juan* from the Spanish Golden Age. In his defence, he had a variety of concerns: most Early English and Restoration plays have large casts, which can mean high financial costs in terms of design and payroll, and 'angels' were noticeably in short supply. In addition to that, he reasoned that with the shadow of Peter Hall looming behind him as Emeritus Director, Shakespeare was, for the time being, 'covered'. If Hall's *Loves Labours Lost* was a mistake, *A Midsummer Night's Dream* in 2010 proved a triumph. Looking back, I think Unwin does consider that he was uncertain about what a Kingston audience might respond to and also that he was too cautious – even if, as when he was in rehearsal for *A Christmas Carol*, he was having to break off for insolvency meetings which might have led to the closure of the theatre and the end of the tale before the play opened.

Unwin did garner many good reviews: as he was getting into his stride, he directed Strindberg's *Miss Julie*. Charles Spencer, in *The Daily Telegraph*, wrote:

> On a midsummer night, Miss Julie, the lady of the big house, comes on strong to her father's valet in the servants' kitchen, teasing him, playing with him, until they have a bitter bout of violent sex which normally takes place off stage but which in Stephen Unwin's fine production is graphically presented before

> the audience … Rachel Pickup as the snobbish, unstable Miss
> Julie, Daniel Betts as the contained, cruel but also subservient
> valet and Lucy Briers as the household's sane and placid cook all
> give performances in Stephen Unwin's production that lucidly
> penetrate the play's dark and feverish heart.

The production played in repertory with Aykbourn's *Bedroom Farce*, directed by Peter Hall. For Hall, it was a return to the play whose premiere he had co-directed at the National over thirty years before. Michael Billington, in reviewing each spoke of Unwin's 'equally good revival' in which 'the dust is swept off an old play through the violent intensity of the acting' (*The Guardian*).

The productions were cross-cast and ran for an eight week season, billed – a little obscurely – as 'behind closed doors'. Some part of the success was owing to Hall's pulling power on actors, as ever assembling a host of well-known players. At other times, Unwin too showed he could attract the best: he already had a history of success with Timothy West, who came to the Rose to play in *The Winslow Boy* and Michael Billington thought 'Unwin's production … is acted with superlative finesse' (*The Guardian*). Celia Imrie played Judith Bliss in Coward's *Hay Fever*, which Charles Spencer hailed as, 'Stephen Unwin's richly enjoyable, beautifully designed revival …' (*Daily Telegraph*), even if Neil Norman was less effusive saying, 'Stephen Unwin's production unwinds with flair if not dedicated precision' (*Daily Express*). Joely Richardson came to the Rose for the first time when she took the lead in *The Lady from the Sea* in 2012 in Unwin's own translation of Ibsen's play. Most critics celebrated the actress's return to the English stage and her courage in taking on a role played previously by both her mother, Vanessa Redgrave, and her sister, Natasha Richardson. However, the reviews were mixed: while the *Evening Standard* found the production 'efficient rather than compelling', and *The Guardian* felt 'Unwin's production needs to push its heroine closer to the edge of madness in order to heighten her triumphant redemption', *The Independent* said that Richardson 'dazzles on her return to the London stage' and that 'Unwin brilliantly unpicks the tangle of nineteenth century relationships'.

These early years were demonstrating several important things: Hall's assertion about the Rose being a special theatre which could combine the epic with the intimate was certainly being manifested, especially in good productions with good players. Some of the country's finest actors wanted to play in Kingston. Nowhere was this more evident than when Judi Dench came to the Rose in early 2010. It was an astonishing and daring decision to take on the role of Titania at the age of seventy five and nearly fifty years after she had first played the part both on stage and in a film each also directed by Hall.

Judi Dench had been associated with the Rose theatre before, in late 2003 contributing her *Judi Dench and Friends* charity night. Before that, she was seen campaigning with Hall to preserve the archaeological foundations on Bankside in 1989, then turning up at a performance of *Romeo and Juliet* (originally *Romeo and Ethel, the Pirate's Daughter*) as Queen Elizabeth 1 in the film *Shakespeare in Love* and winning an Oscar for her efforts. Now she appeared at the Rose as Elizabeth again, in an opening mime licensing the actors to perform, then herself playing the Queen of the Fairies. It was an amusing meta-theatrical trope which itself licensed the succeeding action. The writer and broadcaster Paul Allen, in a special article for the production, asked, 'Are Peter Hall and Judi Dench the Oberon and Titania of the whole of British Theatre? The alchemical mastermind who shaped and ran our greatest companies and the surprisingly skittish actress who can turn the most ordinary material into emotional gold by sheer unforced intensity of feeling?'

In fact the Oberon in this production was Charles Edwards, nearly four decades younger than his Titania. I was delighted to watch this fine, accomplished and self-effacing actor rise to the occasion, as inevitably he would. I had directed Charles as the Earl of Shaftesbury over twenty years before in *The Ragged Child* for the National Youth Music Theatre on stage and on BBC TV. (I also wrote his reference for drama school!) As ever, Hall brought a strong company to the stage, including Rachael Stirling, Julian Wadham, James Laurenson, Susan Salmon, Ben Mansfield, Oliver Chris and Annabel Scholey. He also assembled a team of familiars which included his friend from early RSC days, Elizabeth Bury, as Set and Costume Designer, and long-term collaborators Peter Mumford as Lighting Designer and Mick Sands who wrote the music. Cordelia Monsey, to whom he increasingly turned to for support, was Associate Director.

A Midsummer Night's Dream was a critical triumph and also a hit with the audiences throughout its six week run in February and March 2010. It was a joy to see people queuing around the outside of the Rose for the few tickets available on each day and for the extra performances which were added to the schedule owing to the demand. It was a good production not for any startling innovation, nor even because of Judi Dench: it was a fine example of classical theatre done well. It exemplified everything Hall had written about in his recently published book *Shakespeare's Advice to the Players* which was an expression of his credo. As Hall wrote: 'Shakespeare tells the actor when to go fast and when to go slow, when to pause, when to come in on cue and when to accent a word. His text is full of such clues'. Rehearsals for his productions always began with a textual exploration of discovery which led, at the very least, to textual clarity in performance and *A Midsummer Night's Dream* was no exception. It was the high point of Hall's association with the Rose Theatre, Kingston.

John Thaxter summed this up when he wrote of 'superb verse speaking ... a total respect for Shakespeare's text; a production style that sheds new light on an old familiar play without drawing attention to itself; and a sense of ensemble playing, seamlessly combining sage with tyro while allowing newcomers to emerge as company stars in their own right' (*British Theatre Guide*). Michael Billington initially focused on Judi Dench and her 'supreme ability to give weight to every word she utters'. The question of her age held no problems: 'I've also never seen a Titania more vocally and spiritually enraptured by the transformed Bottom. Dench's voice seems to caress the air as she breathily cries, "I pray thee, gentle mortal, sing again". And, after a night spent with the ass, Dench skips and skitters around with post-coital glee and giggles delightedly at her loved one's every jest. Without any of the physical explicitness you sometimes find in modern productions, Dench simply conveys the ecstasy and ardour of a brief, if misplaced, passion'. And of her (much) younger partner: 'Charles Edwards is a particularly fine Oberon who brings out the sadistic delight with which the fractious immortal torments the fairy queen. He slavers over the idea of streaking her eyes to make her full of "hateful fantasies" and gloats over the prospect of her waking next to some "vile thing". But, in a play that is all about spiritual transfiguration, Edwards conveys a proper sense of guilt at the effectiveness of his ruse' (*The Guardian*).

For Charles Spencer in the *Daily Telegraph* Dench gave 'a performance of wondrous humour and warmth in Peter Hall's delightful production'. Paul Taylor wrote that, 'unfolding on the lozenge-shaped open stage of the Rose Theatre at Kingston, Hall's latest production ... is exquisitely well judged in its light-footed, lucid, poetically persuasive, wonderfully funny and brilliantly well-spoken way' (*The Independent*). Billington concluded his *Guardian* article by returning to Dench: 'That's what I call great acting'.

When, years before, Robin Hutchinson and I had argued for a theatre which fulfilled local aspirations, but which also strived for regional and even national importance we had not fully articulated its possibilities. This was world class theatre.

This happened whilst working to make Rose productions without disappearing into bankruptcy, but also and most importantly with young people. My MA students joined the company of several productions, including *A Midsummer Night's Dream*. They were thrilled to sit in on rehearsals and to play 'walking ladies and gentlemen' and to spend time with ever-generous professionals, including Dame Judi who would take them out to tea.

From the earliest days we were determined that young people should be given the opportunity to have easy and reasonably-priced access to the theatre and this began in the Season in the Shell in 2003, where 'the groundlings' could be closer to the stage than anyone else for the lowest ticket price. After the fit-out, the cheapest seats were on the floor in front of the stage on cushions, for the cost of a cinema ticket and no more. This arrangement was not to everyone's taste, especially when the house was not full. And now it has been superseded with the most expensive seats sited where formerly the groundlings were.

In the very young artistic plans which Robin Hutchinson, Colin Bloxham and I developed in the early nineties we had articulated a desire for an international youth festival: it was one of our fundamental tenets. It was always to be in July: I had an idea, born of my annual sojourns with productions in Edinburgh, that we should precede the Edinburgh Fringe Festival, giving opportunities for new work to come to Kingston for a public try-out, brief enough to qualify productions for Fringe First Awards once they travelled North. When he became Artistic Director, Peter Hall was enthusiastically supportive. At one time Edward Wilson, who had recently left the National Youth Theatre, came to discuss the prospect of running the proposed festival. Sadly, Ed died at a ridiculously young age shortly afterwards. However, once the Rose had opened, we returned to the plan and Kingston's International Youth Arts Festival was born. At the end of 2008, Robin Hutchinson and I held interviews for the role of Festival Director. Colin Chambers prompted us to invite Aniela Zaba, whose MA postgraduate work he had recently externally examined and pronounced exceptional and inventive. Aniela came down to Kingston in late 2008 the night before her interview and, judging by her appearance at the theatre at ten the following morning, had done some experimental festival work into the small hours. It was quickly evident to Robin and me that she combined imaginative invention, wit and ingenuity with an extraordinary stamina, which was to become the hallmark of her years in charge.

There were only a few short months before the inaugural festival in the Summer of 2009 and we were concerned that we might have only a few productions and no control over quality. So I offered with Jo Billington to direct a revival of our NYMT production of *Pendragon* as a sort of benchmark. If we were concerned that the epithet 'International' might be a claim too far, at least initially, we need not have worried. In that first year a company came from the USA and as the years have progressed they have come from all over Europe, from Ireland and from North America.

Having a proven production in that first festival gave us the opportunity to have a Royal Gala performance, as Prince Edward, then the Earl of Wessex, had agreed to become President of Creative Youth, the organising charity behind the festival; he has been unfailing and pro-active in his support of IYAF, now Fuse International, ever since. As with *The Ragged Child* the previous year, we were able to show how effectively young people can perform on the Rose stage. It happens that it also convinced Aretha Ayeh, who played Guinevere in our *Pendragon*, that she should pursue a career in the theatre rather than the law and she is now an established player and RSC actor.

IYAF grew from strength to strength, sustained by Creative Youth, chaired by the ubiquitous Robin Hutchinson. He has, amongst many other characteristics, the ability to inspire and harness the talents of old and young alike – whether Phil Hetherington who retired from public business to head the administration or Andy Currums who succeeded Aniela Zaba within years of graduating from Kingston University's Drama Degree programme. In its first ten years thousands of young people have come to perform from all over the world each July, and the festival has fully reflected Lyn Gardner's suggestion that performances should spill out of the theatre, into the market place and onto the riverbank – and into other, smaller spaces too. It has also amply fulfilled Kingston's desire for a cultural and economic regeneration. Stephen Unwin said that, looking back, IYAF was one of the very important parts of the life of the Rose which he had, initially, underestimated and undervalued.

The emphasis on the work of young people has become a characteristic of Rose life, thanks also in large measure early on to the appointment of Ciaran McConville as Head of Participation and Learning. McConville set about creating a Rose Youth Theatre which actively engages hundreds of young people in its range of training programmes and productions and has become the basis of a series of Christmas shows which are models of creative theatre practice. It says much for the organisation that for several years it entrusted McConville to create and direct productions which, for five or six weeks during December and January, filled the theatre and provided much-needed revenue. In addition to being a director who understands how the Rose works most effectively as a performing space, McConville is a skilled writer and adapter. His creations and re-working of original works, led to fine productions of *A Christmas Carol*, *Toad of Toad Hall*, *Alice in Winterland* and others which have combined professional players in companies which also have large numbers of young people centrally involved. His greatest skill was to showcase, in first class professional productions, the qualities which young people naturally have. On his departure in 2019, McConville left the important impression that the

Rose is a theatre for young people, as well as being a theatre of international quality.

Stephen Unwin concluded a six year tenure as Artistic Director in December 2013. Two years before, Robert O'Dowd had become Chief Executive without any previous experience in theatre and, on Unwin's departure, determined to revamp the way that the Rose was run. He acknowledged that the Rose had given critically acclaimed theatre productions, but it had continued to struggle financially. O'Dowd created a 'business model' based on producer-led theatre. Only a few months previously the Equity President, Malcolm Sinclair, had railed against the Lyric Theatre, Belfast for its decision not to replace its artistic director: 'The Lyric, Belfast, appears to be repeating the idiocy of replacing an artistic director with an executive producer – exactly the same mistake as was made by Hull Truck'. Now Kingston was about to do the same. Initially, O'Dowd said, he would try the model for eighteen months or so. The Rose went 'in house' for its Producer. Jerry Gunn had had a breadth of experience for nearly thirty years in theatre and was in 2013 the General Manager of the Rose. Having been educated in Kingston, he came back as Company Manager and Stage Manager for the Peter Hall Company in 2004. Gunn also had experience in Opera, Music Theatre and Classical Theatre in a range of technical and administrative roles. In January 2014 he became the Executive Producer of the Rose: it proved to be a very important appointment.

If the Rose was now on a much more sound financial footing, a glance at some of the highlights of the five years following Unwin's departure suggests that production values remained high. Some productions were Rose only shows, whilst others were co-productions with theatres such as Sheffield Theatres or Bristol Old Vic and sometimes with companies such as English Touring Theatre. There was no shortage of directors wanting to create productions for the Rose: Trevor Nunn, Sally Cookson, Melly Still, John Malkovich, Lindsay Posner, Simon Goodwin, James Grieve and Jeremy Herrin indicate the calibre which could be brought to a lovely theatre.

Translations was an early success under this new regime, directed by James Grieve and in collaboration with English Touring Theatre and

Sheffield Theatres (where it was reviewed). Alfred Hickling thought it, 'an exemplary revival by James Grieve of what is arguably [Friel's] greatest play' (*The Guardian*). Jacqueline Wilson is Kingston's own internationally renowned novelist and it was appropriate that a dramatisation of her *Hetty Feather* should be an early Rose production and it was a triumph. Following her brilliant production of *Jane Eyre* at the Bristol Old Vic, Sally Cookson directed, with Phoebe Thomas as Hetty and young audiences were captivated, as were the critics. After a sell-out run at the Rose, off it went on tour around the country and into the West End to the Vaudeville Theatre. In a novel turn Jacquie Wilson wrote her own review in *The Guardian*: 'Seeing the stage version alongside hundreds of children on the edges of their seats was a magical experience. [Hetty] became totally real to all of us. I can't wait to go again'. Holly Williams in *The Independent* reflected the overwhelming critical approval: 'Wilson's plot makes a strong case for the power of invention and the magic of storytelling – both of which the production spectacularly delivers on'.

Perhaps the production that has best epitomised the potential that the Rose has as a place of classical theatre was *The Wars of the Roses* in 2015. Robert O'Dowd rightly described it as our 'biggest and most ambitious project to date ...' It coincided with Chris Foy becoming Chair of the Trustees and so was something of a watershed moment, following the years of Anthony Simonds-Gooding, whose legacy was some financial security.

In the early years of the Royal Shakespeare Company, at Peter Hall's instigation, Shakespeare's four early history plays – *Henry V1 Parts 1,2 and 3* and *Richard 111* – were adapted by John Barton into three plays, *Henry V1, Edward 1V and Richard 111* and presented as *The Wars of the Roses*. They were directed by Barton and Hall, opening in Stratford in 1963. It is difficult to exaggerate the impact that they made then and the BBC began one of its most ambitious arts projects when it filmed the productions for broadcast in April 1965. I vividly remember those black and white images: of David Warner as Henry V1, sitting alone in his long white robes as the Battle of Tewkesbury raged; of close-ups of Ian Holm as Richard, quietly and without theatricality scheming. Between the Stratford productions and the televised performances a young Trevor Nunn came to the RSC.

As he was preparing his own production fifty years later at the Rose, Nunn reflected on his early experience with Hall and Barton: 'I was privileged to become a close colleague and friend of both men, and had the amazing good fortune to have them as my mentors, teachers and inspiration. So I want to shout their names from the rooftops. I want to celebrate Peter as the most original, accomplished director/impresario of the twentieth century; and John, the single most influential figure in the speaking and inhabiting of Shakespeare's verse on stage'.

Hall's own words, written for the BBC forty five years earlier, captured the plays' continuing relevance: 'Over the years I became more and more fascinated by the contortions of politicians, and by the corrupting seductions of anybody who wields power. I began to collect "sanctions" – those justifications which politicians use in the press or on television to mask the dictates of their party politics or their personal ambitions: "not in the public interest"; "the country is not ready for it"; "the man in the street will never accept …"; "let me say quite frankly …"' They are eternally relevant thoughts.

Nunn called on the great designer, John Napier, a veteran of such other epic productions as *Nicholas Nickleby* for the RSC. Writing in *A Younger Theatre*, Holly O'Mahony captured its quality: 'The set, designed for the Rose by John Napier and Mark Friend, is a graceful bow to the original Rose Playhouse. Simple wooden planks and stairwells frame the back of the stage, with candles peeking out between the swords and shields hung across the walls … With a cast of 23 professional actors and a further 30 youth theatre and community chorus members, *The Wars of the Roses* is an ambitious, thorough and lovingly crafted production – fine-tuned and accessible to seasoned and fresh-faced audiences alike'.

The pity was that the cast lacked ethnic diversity and Nunn's defence sadly missed the mark, mumbling about authenticity. Shakespeare's iambic line is inauthentic, but we do not transpose it back to a language spoken in the fifteenth century. Did this give Susannah Clapp cause to damn the performances in *The Observer*? 'Nunn's production, rightly criticised for its all-whiteness, presents a group of pop-up greats, gilded figures, some dashingly performed, who wrangle with each other in a vacuum. The scenes with "the poor" are terrible. Dun-coloured peasants, drooping under those depressing hats with dangly bits at the sides, slump at the same time, roar in the same way and make identical gestures … Nine hours is a long time for a tribute pageant. Surely the best way of honouring a theatrical revolution is a new revolt'.

By contrast in the sister paper Clapp's colleague Michael Billington wrote 'although Nunn sees the production as a tribute to his twin mentors at the RSC, it exists as a thrilling piece of theatre in its own right … I won't deny there were moments when my own vision was overlaid by memories of the past but they were banished by Nunn's priceless ability to refashion these plays for our own divided age' (*The Guardian*). A fine cast featured Alexandra Gilbreath, Joely Richardson, Alex Hanson, Kare Conradi, Rufus Hound, Alex Waldmann (who drew a relenting note from Susanah Clapp: 'when was Henry VI so interesting? Alex Waldmann makes him fresh, strange and convincing') and Robert Sheahan.

Paul Taylor in *The Independent* found it a 'wonderfully engrossing production', while Dominic Cavendish in *The Daily Telegraph* wrote: 'By the riverside at Kingston upon Thames, theatrical history is being remade. *The Wars of the Roses* was the crowning glory of the early years of the RSC, lending it vital legitimacy. Now it has been set upon the stage for the first time since 1963: a colossal undertaking, and a high-risk one … deploying a dynamic 23-strong cast, his exhilarating production not only gives the RSC a run for its money, it pays poignant tribute to the now ailing pair and their landmark legacy … this is gripping, courageous, essential. And sure to inspire a new generation'.

After the opening night, Trevor Nunn stood on the stage and said, 'I have just five words: Peter Hall and John Barton'. It was a tribute to two theatrical campaigners, who were both to die within a few months of each other less than three years later. For me, it justified Hall's confidence in the versatility of our new Rose and also the line which he happily confessed to having borrowed from Nunn that 'this is the playhouse I have dreamed of all my life'. It is, after all, a modern playhouse which honours one which thrived over four hundred years ago.

When she next came to the Rose – as the national critics now did routinely – Susannah Clapp had no reservations. It was to see *Good Canary*, directed by John Malkovich and with a cast including Freya

Mavor and Harry Lloyd: 'The Rose at Kingston has suddenly bloomed. John Malkovich's production of *Good Canary* makes much of London theatre look slow-witted and slow-eyed'. Zach Helm's play, written only a decade earlier and in its first English language version at the Rose had a brilliant design by Pierre-Francois Limbosch: the latter saw the potential of the Rose stage to use projection and this allowed Malkovich to move from reality to a kind of surreality, by means of Limbosch's rich scenic projections and some skilful acting performances. I have never seen a more effective and affecting depiction of drug addiction on the stage.

These two very different productions, *The Wars of the Roses* and *Good Canary*, demonstrated how effective the 'producer-led' model could be – provided, of course, that the producer is of Jerry Gunn's imagination and authority, supported by a Chief Executive (Robert O'Dowd) and a Chair (Chris Foy) and a Board of Trustees who will accept that there are risks in making such different projects in the theatre. Each production boasted distinguished but contrasting directors, designers and casts. The most telling contrast was in the nature of the dramatic material and the common element is a unique theatre which is able to embody such creative, diverse and versatile dramatic endeavour. Could this approach be sustained without the over-arching unifying vision of an artistic director?

Meanwhile, the Rose was demonstrating to itself and Kingston University another potential. Richard Wilson had joined the University in 2012 as the Peter Hall Professor of Shakespeare Studies. He created the Kingston Shakespeare Seminars at the Rose and convened a series of major international conferences which attracted distinguished Shakespeareans from around the world. *Marlowe and Shakespeare*, in November 2017, attracted a host of scholars, including Charles Nicholl, Lois Potter, Jean Howard and Stanley Wells to the Rose. Gary Taylor and Brian Vickers were given the opportunity to reopen an on-going argument about authorship. *Barton, Hall and Shakespeare*, in September 2018, assessed the work of two of the twentieth century's greatest practitioners with contributions from scholars, such as Michael Dobson, as well as actors and directors from such as Judi Dench, Janet Suzman, Trevor Nunn and Michael Pennington. Thus the Rose, which was proving to be such a fine theatre became also a focus for research and learning.

Any theatre needs constant renewal, which comes from the human reflections and endeavours of directors, actors, writers, designers, administrators and audiences. The Rose on Bankside was born in 1587 and thrilled audiences for almost sixteen years before it closed suddenly in 1603, to be forgotten as it slipped down into the Thames mud. It re-emerged in 1989, where it is more than a ghost, a trace, as the Rose Playhouse, Bankside, but also to be the inspiration for the Rose of Kingston. Our theatre has already lasted for longer than its precursor, and has embodied much human spirit and aspiration, but it is a fragile thing, to be nurtured and cherished by people who must be alert to the whims of social, political and economic change. And, as we learned from 2020, the potential ravages of a global pandemic.

Afterword

One of the most powerful theatrical alliances was formed when Edward Alleyn married Joan Woodward, the stepdaughter of Philip Henslowe, in October 1592. At the end of January 1593 the Queen's Privy Council issued a restraint, effectively an order to close the London theatres in the face of the worst outbreak of plague since the Black Death had ravaged the country in 1348. For ten months, up until the following December, Henslowe had to close the Rose as the city went into lockdown. Edward Alleyn left both London and his new wife Joan and took his actors, the Admiral's Men, away from the capital to play in the provinces.

When Christopher Haydon was appointed Artistic Director of the Rose Theatre, Kingston in October 2019 he said, 'The Rose has established itself as a contemporary home for thrilling and ambitious theatre and I am delighted to be its new Artistic Director. I can't wait to begin steering this amazing building into the future'. But wait he had to do: a plague lay ready to blight Haydon's ambitions. On 16th March 2020 the government imposed restrictions on theatres owing to the rapidly spreading coronavirus and the Rose made the announcement that 'all shows and events at the Rose starting from today, Tuesday 17th March, will be suspended until further notice …' A list of postponements and cancellations ran on for much of the next eighteen months. At last, in September 2021 Haydon's first production, *Leopards*, a new play by Alys Metcalf opened and there were audible sighs of relief. A new era had begun.

Index